Marionetten
Kunst, Bau, Spiel

Marionettes
Art, Construction, Play

Zum Schauen, Lesen, Träumen,
vielleicht an einem trüben Regentag,
an dem die Sonne scheinen soll ...

For looking, reading, dreaming,
perhaps on a grey, rainy day,
to make the sun shine ...

Marlene Gmelin
Detlef Schmelz

Marionetten

Kunst, Bau, Spiel

Marionettes

Art, Construction, Play

Swiridoff Verlag

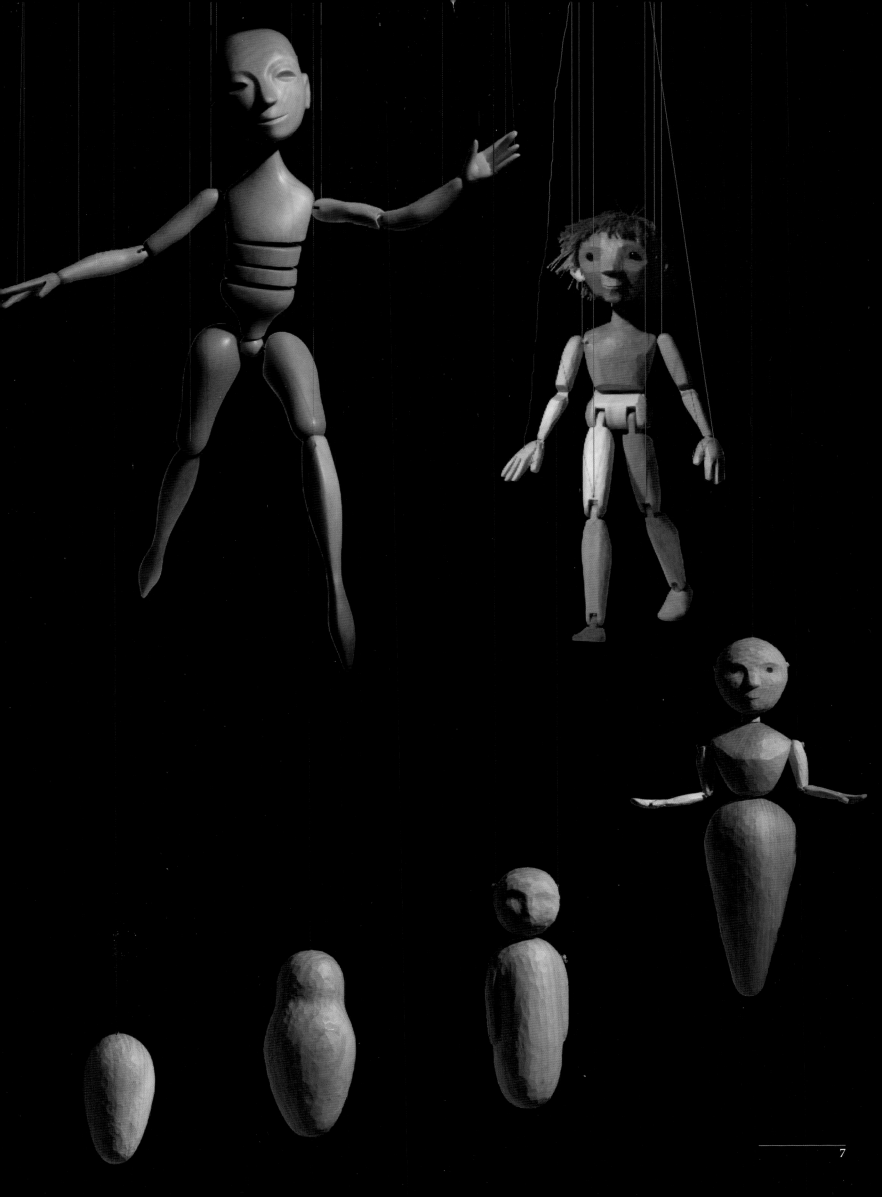

Pendel-Marionetten

Pendel Marionettes

Dieses Buch erzählt von der Marionette als Kunst- und Spielfigur – wie sie entsteht und wie sie sich bewegt. Mit ihr beschäftigen wir uns seit nunmehr vierzig Jahren. Schon während unseres Studiums bauten wir Marionetten und gründeten ein Studententheater. Darüber lernten wir die Koryphäe auf diesem Gebiet, Fritz Herbert Bross, kennen. Von ihm und einem seiner Schüler lernten wir viel über das komplexe, oft geheim gehaltene Wissen über den Bau der Marionette und das Spiel mit ihr. Unsere Arbeit fußt im Wesentlichen auf vier Säulen:

Der Marionettenbau
Wir bauen sehr bewegliche und ausdrucksstarke Marionetten für all diejenigen, die mit professionellen Marionetten spielen möchten. Ein einfach zu handhabendes Spielkreuz und eine ausgeklügelte Gelenktechnik verhelfen den Figuren zu verblüffend natürlichen Bewegungsabläufen. Auch für den Laien sind sie spielend zu bewegen. Einige unserer Figuren bekamen international renommierte Preise.

Das Marionettentheater
Als Theater bevorzugen wir das pantomimische Spiel. Durch das sprachfreie Spiel konnten wir in vielen Ländern und Kontinenten auftreten. Wir bieten des Weiteren Inszenierungen von Märchen, Mythen und Fantasiegeschichten, doch auch hier steht das gesprochene Wort im Hintergrund. Unser kleines stationäres Theater in Hermuthausen bei Künzelsau gilt in der Region als Geheimtipp. Als Tourneetheater treten wir im In- und Ausland auf.
In unserer vielschichtigen, poetischen Spielweise wenden wir uns an das Kind im Menschen.

This book is all about marionettes – both as objects of art and theatre figures – and how they are created and move. Marionettes have now been part of our lives for forty years. While still students, we began making marionettes, which then led on to the creation of a student theatre. Through this, we got to know Fritz Herbert Bross, one of the giants of marionette theatre. From him and one of his students, we acquired much of the complex and often arcane knowledge about how to make and play marionettes. Our work now mainly rests on four pillars:

Marionette making
We make highly mobile and highly expressive marionettes for all those wanting to work with professional marionettes. An easily handled control bar and the carefully crafted joints enable the figures to perform astonishingly natural movements. They are very simple to operate, even by amateurs. Some of our figures have been awarded internationally renowned prizes.

The marionette theatre
As a theatre, we prefer to work in mime and have therefore been able to play in many countries on many continents. We also offer productions based on fairy stories, myths and fantasy tales, but even in this case, the spoken word tends to play a secondary role. Our small, permanent theatre in Hermuthausen near Künzelsau is highly renowned in the local region. When on tour, we play at bigger venues both in Germany and abroad.
Through the multifaceted nature of our productions and our poetic style, we appeal to the child in people.

The marionette playing courses
For many years now, we have offered courses in marionette playing in Hohebuch, Baden-Württemberg. Over the years, these courses have led to the creation of various marionette theatres in Germany and neighbouring countries. Covering a wide diversity, many of them perform to a very high standard – in all cases using our marionettes. From this, it was only one step more to crown the courses with the Pendel-Marionette-Festival, Hohebuch.

Die Marionettenspielkurse

Seit vielen Jahren unterrichten wir das Marionettenspiel in einem Seminarhaus in Waldenburg-Hohebuch, Baden-Württemberg. Mit der Zeit entstanden aus dieser Kurstätigkeit zahlreiche Marionettentheater in Deutschland und den Nachbarländern, die sehr variantenreich und oft auf hohem Niveau spielen – immer mit unseren Marionetten. So lag es nahe, als Krönung der Spielkurse das Pendel-Marionettenfestival, Hohebuch zu veranstalten. Seit 2008 zeigt es alle zwei Jahre eindrücklich den Zauber und die Vielfalt des Marionettenspiels.

Die Marionettenfilme

Als jüngste Projekte kamen Marionettenspielfilme hinzu. Zurzeit entsteht ein Kinofilm über den Umgang von uns Menschen mit der Umwelt und die Folgen für das Klima.

Von alledem soll dieses Buch berichten und zeigen, wie unendlich vielschichtig die Marionette ist.

Physikalisch betrachtet ist die Marionette ein Pendel. Auf der Suche nach einem Namen für uns und unser Theater fanden wir daher die Bezeichnung „Pendel" sehr treffend. In diesem Namen drückt sich unsere langjährige Beschäftigung mit der Marionette aus; gleichzeitig ist er ein Symbol für unsere Beziehung: Während ihrer Entstehung schwingt die Marionette zwischen uns hin und her, pendelt mal weit in den Bereich des anderen hinein, um wieder zurückzukommen und doch gleich wieder zu gehen. Sie entsteht in einer andauernden Auseinandersetzung mit der Arbeit des Partners und entwickelt sich dabei mit einer gewissen Eigendynamik zu einer eigenen Persönlichkeit.
Unser Logo zeigt eine stilisierte Blattlaus als Pendel.

Since 2008, this has been held every two years and is an excellent platform for presenting all the magic and variety of marionette theatre.

The marionette films

As our latest project, we have ventured into the field of marionette films. We are currently making a film that deals with how we humans treat the environment and how this affects the climate.

The aim of this book is to tell more about all of this and to show how infinitely rich and diverse the world of marionettes can be.

In practical terms, a marionette is a form of pendulum. So when searching for a name for ourselves and our theatre, we found the term "Pendel" – the German word for "pendulum" – appropriate. This name reflects our long-standing occupation with marionettes, but also stands as a symbol of the relationship between us: In the course of its creation, a marionette passes back and forth between us, sometimes swinging far into the realm of the other, only to return but then turn round and go off again. Each marionette is the result of a continuous process of dialogue with the work of the other partner, but thanks to a certain innate momentum, it also develops a personality of its own. Our logo is therefore a stylized greenfly in a pendulum.

Marlene Gmelin und Detlef Schmelz

www.pendel-marionetten.de

Die Sonne strahlt die größte Energie aus. Als kosmischer Feuerball erhellt sie und erwärmt sie unsere Erde und ermöglicht dadurch alles Leben. Aber wenn man ihr zu nahe kommt, blendet, versengt und verbrennt sie uns und unsere Lebensgrundlagen. Sie ist die Herrscherin über den Tag.

The sun radiates more energy than anything else. This cosmic fireball lights up and warms our world and thereby makes possible all life on earth. But if you venture too close to it, it blinds, singes and burns us up and the things that keep us alive. It is the ruler of our days.

In der Nacht, wenn die Mondin ihr sanftes
Licht vom Himmel zur Erde schickt, besinnt
sich der Mensch auf sich selbst.
Es währt die Zeit der Innerlichkeit.

At night, when the moon casts down its soft
light on the earth from the sky, mankind is
inwardly reflective.
This is the time for introspection.

die ist die Leben hervorbringende, sich ständig erneuernde Naturkraft, das Symbol des Ganzen. Sie ist der mütterliche Urschoß, in dem alles entsteht, und der Grabschoß, in den alles Entstandene wieder zurücksinkt. Obwohl in stetigem Wandel, ist die Erde beständig. Sie lässt Gutes und Böses zu.
Alles Geschehen hat seine Berechtigung.

This is the ever regenerative power of nature which produces life. It is the symbol of completeness. It is the maternal womb creating all life and the lap of the grave to which all created life must return. Although it is in a state of permanent change, earth is enduring. It allows good as it does evil
All happenings have their justification.

Das Feuer

Es verkörpert die flammende Lebensenergie. Es wärmt und schützt und vermittelt dadurch das Gefühl des Aufgehobenseins in einer Gemeinschaft. Es gilt als Wandlungs- und Läuterungssymbol: Materie wird durch Hitze in eine andere Form gebracht, Elemente werden getrennt oder verschmolzen. Das Feuer reinigt und reduziert auf das Wesentliche.

Fire

Fire embodies the fiery energy of life. It warms and protects and as a result, provides feeling of disconnected existence in a community. It is considered to be the symbol of transformation and purification. Matter brought by heat into another form, elements are separated or merged. Fire cleanses and reduces to the essentials.

Das Wasser

Das Wasser gilt als die Quelle der Lebenskraft, es ist das Symbol für die Seelenwelten.
Es charakterisiert sich durch Beweglichkeit, Bewegung und Bewegtsein.

The Water

Water is deemed to be the source of vitality, it is the symbol for the world of souls.
It is characterised by mobility, movement and animation.

Der Regen
Des Menschen Seele gleicht dem Wasser:
Vom Himmel kommt es, zum Himmel steigt es,
und wieder nieder zur Erde muss es,
ewig wechselnd.
Johann Wolfgang von Goethe

The Rain
The human soul is like water:
It comes from heaven, it aspires to heaven.
and must return to earth once more,
eternally alternating.
Johann Wolfgang von Goethe

Der Westwind kommt über
den Atlantik und bringt uns
die Regenwolken als lebens-
spendendes Nass.

The west wind blows over the
Atlantic and brings us rain clouds
to release life-giving moisture.

Die Luft
Die Luft ist wie eine zärtliche Berührung vom
Unsichtbaren her. Sie kommt aus dem Bereich
des Irrationalen, äußert sich in schöpferischen
Ideen und vermittelt uns Gefühle von Leichtigkeit, Inspiration und Freiheit. Sie verbindet
alles mit allem. Sie trägt Düfte, Töne, Teilchen
und hält damit die Welt in Bewegung.

Der Südwind bringt uns die
warme Brise, die wir genießen
und die uns anspornt zu vielen
Aktivitäten. Aber er ist auch der Meister
der sengenden Hitze und der Gewitter-
stürme.

The south wind brings us warm breezes which
we enjoy and which are an incentive to be
active. But it is also master of
parching heat and thunder storms.

The air

The air is like a tender caress by the invisible.
It comes from the sphere of the irrational, and
expresses itself in creative ideas and imparts
feelings of lightness, inspiration and freedom to
us. Air connects everything with everything. It
bears fragrances, musical tones, particles thereby making the world go round..

Der Nordwind kommt stampfend
von Grönland her.
Er gebietet über Hagel, Schnee
und eisige Regenschauer.

The north wind comes bearing
down on us from Greenland.
It is lord and master of hail,
snow and icy rain showers.

Die Heimat des Ostwindes ist die Mongolei.
Er bringt uns trockenes, heißes Wetter im Sommer
oder schneidende Kälte im Winter.

Mongolia is the home of the east wind.
It brings us dry hot weather in summer or
bitter cold weather in winter.

Bewegte Kunst

Moving art

Unendlich vielschichtig

Die „kleine Marie" an Fäden, gemeinhin Marionette genannt, übt auf viele Menschen eine große, magische Anziehungskraft aus. In diesem
geheimnisvollen Wesen steckt viel mehr Tiefe,
als man auf den ersten Blick vermutet.

Die Marionette vereint auf einzigartige Weise
Handwerk und Kunst. Sie verbindet bildende
und darstellende Kunst. Am Anfang steht die
handwerkliche Ausführung – in Holz, Metall
und Textil. Der präzise, von der Anatomie
abgeleitete Aufbau gibt der Marionette ihre
natürlich wirkenden Bewegungen. Doch vor
allem durch die künstlerische Ausgestaltung
entfaltet die Marionette ihre Wirkung auf den
Betrachter. Schon in Ruhe macht die bewegliche Skulptur einen starken Eindruck. Animiert
durch den Spieler, verstärkt sich der ihr inne-
wohnende Ausdruck. Sie berührt den Zuschauer in seiner Seele.

Figures with many facets

Marionettes exert a powerful, magical fascina-
tion on many people. Meaning "Little Mary"
and named after the Holy Virgin, these enigmatic beings have much greater depth than might
be assumed at first sight.

Marionettes represent a unique amalgamation
of manual craftsmanship and art. They combine both visual and performing arts. The first
step is the actual physical creation of the figures – using wood, metal and textiles. In terms of
practical construction, they follow the anatomy
of the being they represent, and it is this that
gives them their show of natural movement.
But more than anything, it is the artistic appearance that makes the impact on the audience.
Already at rest, this mobile sculpture can make
a powerful impression on the viewer. Animated
by the player, the inherent expressiveness takes
on a new dimension, with the ability to touch
the spectators to their very soul.

Kleine Marie
Der Begriff Ma
rionette ist frar
zösischen Ur-
sprungs, ver-
mutlich ent-
standen aus de
Verkleinerungs
form von Marie
Figuren, die di
Mutter Maria
und andere He
lige darstellten
waren mit Me-
chanismen aus
gestattet und
konnten sich
deshalb schein
bar von selbst
bewegen.

Little Mary
Marionette is a
word of French
origin, presum
bly a diminutiv
form of Marie,
or Mary. Figure
depicting the
Virgin Mary
and other saint
were equipped
with mecha-
nisms which
were intended
to make them
look as if they
were moving
of their own
accord.

Die Kunst des Marionettenspiels

Das Geheimnis der Marionette

Die Marionette ist die einzige Theaterfigur, die sich scheinbar frei und losgelöst von dem sie führenden Spieler bewegt. Dank der Fäden ist sie ein Wesen der Luft und braucht den Boden nur, um die Schwerkraft darzustellen. Sie wirkt eigenständig und lebendig – voller Anmut und Grazie.

Neben einer gelungenen äußeren Gestaltung sind es drei „innere Werte", die eine gut spielbare Marionette ausmachen. Zum einen liegen

Zudem haben diese Puppen
den Vorteil, dass sie antigrav* sind.
Von der Trägheit der Masse, dieser
dem Tanze entgegenstrebendsten
aller Eigenschaften, wissen sie nichts:
weil die Kraft, die sie in die Lüfte erhebt,
größer ist als jene, die sie an die Erde fesselt ...

Heinrich von Kleist
* unabhängig von der Schwerkraft

ihre Schwerpunkte an den anatomisch richtigen Stellen. Weiterhin entsprechen ihre Gelenke in Funktion und Bewegungsumfang der Anatomie ihres Vorbildes. Und schließlich setzen Spielkreuz und Fäden die Impulse des Spielers effektiv um.

Je konsequenter der Marionettenbildner dies umsetzt, desto natürlicher werden die Bewegungen der Marionette. Dabei verbindet er ebenso filigranes wie solides Handwerk mit ausdrucksstarker, auf das Wesentliche reduzierter Kunst. So wie die Geige zum Erklingen von Tönen gebaut ist, fertigt der Marionettenbildner sein „Instrument" für die Bewegung und den Ausdruck. Sie ist eine Theaterfigur. Erst im Spiel mit ihr offenbart sich das Können des Marionettenbildners.

The art of marionetteering

The secret of marionettes

The marionette is the only theatrical figure that appears to move completely freely and separately from the person behind it. Thanks to the strings, it is an aerial being, only needing the ground to indicate the force of gravity. Imbued with grace and dignity, it appears to have a life and personality of its own.

Aside from the actual physical appearance of the figure, it is the three "hidden values" that make for a well-performing marionette. The first is that the centre of gravity is always located in the anatomically correct place. The second is that the joints of the marionette correspond in function and scope of movement to the anatomy of the real-life being on which it is modelled. And finally, that the control bar and strings effectively transmit the impulses given by the player.

The more successful the marionette maker is in achieving these requirements, the more natural the marionette's movements will be. The task of the maker is to combine filigree but

These puppets have the additional advantage
of being antigrave*.
They know nothing of the inertia of mass,
that property which is the most inimical to dance
as the force that lifts them into the air
is stronger than that which fetters them
to the ground...

Heinrich von Kleist
* independent of gravity

robust handicraft with artwork that is reduced to the essentials while still remaining highly expressive. As a violin is made for producing sound, the marionette is an instrument made for creating movement and expression. It is a theatrical figure. The skill of the marionette maker only fully reveals itself when the figure is actually played.

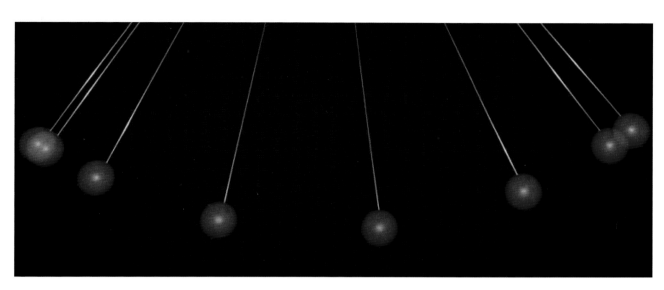

Die Marionette als Pendelsystem

Da die Marionette an Fäden hängt, wird sie –
physikalisch betrachtet – zum Pendel und besitzt dessen Eigenschaften. Anhand einer Kugel
am Faden kann man sich verdeutlichen, welche Kräfte wirken und welche Möglichkeiten
sich ergeben. In der Ruhelage, wenn nur die
Schwerkraft wirkt, hängt sie senkrecht unter
ihrem Aufhängepunkt. Wird die Kugel ange-
stoßen, wirkt die Fliehkraft und der ehemalige
Ruhepunkt wird zum Ort der größten Unruhe, zum Ort der höchsten Geschwindigkeit.
Es ist unmöglich, das Pendel hier zu stoppen.
Je länger der Faden ist, desto größer ist der
Ausschlag und der Moment der Bewegung,
der Freiheit, der Unkontrolliertheit. An den
Endpunkten des Ausschlags, wo es seine Be-
wegungsrichtung ändert, kommt das Pendel
für einen kurzen Moment zum Stillstand. Nur
hier und jetzt kann der Spieler das Pendel zur
Ruhe und damit wieder unter seine Kontrolle
bringen.

The marionette – a pendulum system

A marionette is suspended on strings. Physically speaking, therefore, it is a pendulum,
with all the properties of a pendulum. Through
a weight attached to a string, it is possible to
illustrate the forces that are at work, but also
the potential that is available. At rest, when the
only force acting is gravity, the weight hangs
vertically below the point of suspension. If the
weight is set in motion, however, centrifugal
force takes over, and the former point of rest
becomes the site of the greatest unrest and the
point of greatest velocity.
It is impossible to stop the pendulum at that
point. And the longer the string, the greater is
also the extent of swing and the moment of movement, freedom and lack of control. At the end
of each swing, where the direction of motion
changes, the pendulum comes to a standstill for
a brief moment. Only at this point in space and
time is the player able to stop the pendulum
and bring it back under his control.

Man kommt
nicht umhin,
sich mit den
Pendelgesetzen
zu befassen,
wenn man eine
Marionette ru-
hig und sicher
führen will.
Anhand einer
Kugel an einem
Faden lässt sich
alles Wesentli-
che darstellen
und erklären.

Anyone wan-
ting to handle
a marionette
smoothly and
with assurance
has to be fami-
liar with the
pendulum laws.
It is possible
to illustrate
and explain
these with a ball
suspended on a
string.

Das Beherrschen des Pendelsystems

Der Marionettenspieler ist bestrebt, die Bewegungen der Figur zu jedem Zeitpunkt zu kontrollieren. Deshalb führt er sie so, dass sie sich senkrecht und stabil unter dem Spielkreuz befindet und nicht in seitliche Schwingungen, ins Pendeln, gerät. Die Marionette besteht jedoch nicht aus einem einzigen Pendel. Sie besitzt neben dem Rumpf auch Arme, Beine und einen Kopf. Das Spiel mit der Marionette ist demzufolge das Beherrschen eines Systems von miteinander verbundenen Pendeln – ein „Mobile aus mehreren Kugeln", das sich laufend verändert – in Gestalt eines Menschen. Der Spieler führt das Mobile so, dass er es in jedem Moment stoppen kann, ohne dass einzelne Pendel nachschwingen.

Im Vergleich zur Hand- oder Stabpuppe ist das Führen der Marionette höchst indirekt. Ein oben ausgelöster Impuls kommt verzögert und oftmals verändert unten an. Er wird beeinflusst von anderen vorher oder nachher gegebenen Impulsen. Dadurch können einzelne Pendel in Unruhe geraten. Nur durch direktes und schnelles Reagieren bleibt die Figur in ihren Bewegungen stabil. Und die Zuschauer behalten die Illusion, dass es sich um ein eigenständiges Wesen handelt. Der Spieler lernt, mit solch schwierigen Situationen umzugehen. Er jongliert sozusagen mit Pendeln und ist bestrebt, diese unter Kontrolle zu halten. Er begreift dabei, dass Logik und Mechanik das Marionettenspiel bestimmen.

Die Marionette als Spiegel des Spielers

Um die Marionette führen zu können, befasst sich der Spieler mit Gestik und ganz allgemein mit der menschlichen Bewegung. Fragen wie „Wie bewege ich mich beim Laufen?", „Wie setze ich mich hin?", „Wie stehe ich auf?" werden durch die Beobachtung seiner eigenen Bewegungen beantwortet. „Wie drücke ich eine Hinwendung, wie eine Ablehnung aus?" Solche Fragen führen auf eine Reise zu sich selbst. Der eigene Körper wird zum Lehrer.

Der Spieler schenkt der Figur Leben. Er führt sie, und gleichzeitig dient er ihr. Er denkt sich in ihr Wesen hinein. Er spielt sie dann überzeugend, wenn er die Welt mit ihren Augen erlebt, an ihrer Stelle denkt, fühlt und handelt.

Control of the pendulum system

The aim of the puppeteer is to control the movements of the marionette at all times. He therefore ensures that it is stably positioned directly beneath the control bar and does not start to swing to and fro, like a pendulum. However, a marionette does not constitute just a single pendulum. As well as the trunk, the figure also has arms, legs and a head. Playing a marionette therefore means controlling a system of connected pendulums in the form of a human figure – a constantly changing mobile comprising several "weights". The player must handle the mobile in such a way that it can be brought to a standstill at any time, with none of the pendulums continuing to swing.

Compared to a hand or rod puppet, handling a marionette is a very indirect process. An impulse initiated from above may arrive with a delay or not as intended, being affected along the way by other impulses given earlier or later. This can set individual pendulums in motion.

Jonglieren mit Pendeln – nur durch schnelles Reagieren bleibt die Marionette in ihren Bewegungen stabil.

Juggling with pendulums – only quick responses can keep the movements of a marionette stable.

Die enge Beziehung zwischen Spieler und Marionette spiegelt sich im Körper des Spielers wider.

So kommt es, dass bei expressiven Bewegungen wie dem Tanz auch der Spieler „tanzt".

Wenn alles klappt, ist ein Mobile ein Stück Poesie, das vor Lebensfreude tanzt.

Alexander Calder

Alexander Calder, der sich Zeit seines Lebens mit kinetischer Kunst auseinander setzte, sagte: „Wenn alles klappt, ist ein Mobile ein Stück Poesie, das vor Lebensfreude tanzt." Marionettenspiel ist kinetische Kunst und der Spieler ist Teil des Kunstwerks. Das Prinzip des Pendels wirkt innerhalb der Figur ebenso wie zwischen ihr und dem Spieler in einem lebendigen Hin und Her.

Only a rapid, direct reaction can keep the figure stable. The player's ability to manage situations of this kind improves constantly. For him, it is a case of juggling with the pendulums and striving to keep them under control. Handling a marionette is a matter of logic and mechanics.

The marionette – a mirror of the player's soul
In order to handle a marionette, the puppeteer must be familiar with all manner of gestures and with human movement in general. Questions like "How do I move my body when running?", "How do I sit down?" or "How do I stand up?" can be answered by observing his own movements. "How do I express affection, or rejection?" Such questions as this are the start of a journey to one's own self. The puppeteer's own body becomes the teacher. The player breathes life into the figure. While it is true that he manipulates it, he is also its servant. He puts himself in the marionette's place. He plays it most convincingly when he sees the

Das Zusammenspiel von Spieler und Marionette

Nicht immer macht die Marionette genau die Bewegungen, die der Spieler erzielen will. Er kann dann entweder einen Gegenimpuls einleiten, um die beabsichtigten Bewegungen zu erzwingen, oder er lässt sich von der Marionette leiten, greift deren Bewegungen auf und integriert sie in sein Spiel. Das ist oft die klügere Entscheidung. Denn in solchen Momenten unbeabsichtigten Spiels liegt viel kreatives Potenzial. Es fordert den Spieler zur intuitiven Reaktion. Er spürt in seinem Instrument ein lebendiges, starkes Gegenüber und lernt, ein gewisses Eigenleben seiner Marionette zu tolerieren. Ein virtuoses Pingpong kann entstehen, wenn Spieler und Figur interagieren. Die Figur

... spielt der Marionettenkünstler auch mit den Dingen selbst, so als wären sie lebendig. Er benutzt sie als poetisches Instrument. Das Surreale ist eine große Möglichkeit dieses Spiels.
Marcel Marceau

kann sich dabei als so eigenständig erweisen, dass sie dem Spieler für kurze, glückliche Momente das Heft aus der Hand nimmt und ihn führt. Wenn er dann den Mut hat, sich von ihr leiten zu lassen, entstehen geniale Situationen, auf die der Spieler von allein niemals gekommen wäre. Es zeigt sich dann, dass er nicht der allein Bestimmende, sondern vielmehr der animierende Dienende ist. Er beseelt die Marionette. Er ist mit seinen Sinnen in ihr und durchlebt das, was die Figur vorgibt zu erleben. Und manchmal ist unklar, wer wen führt.

world through its eyes, when he thinks, feels and acts as it does.
The close relationship between the player and marionette is also reflected in the player's body. Consequently, in the case of expressive movements such as dancing, it happens that the puppeteer also "dances".

When everything goes right, a mobile is a piece of poetry that dances with the joy of life.
Alexander Calder

Alexander Calder, who said this, worked intensely with kinetic art. Marionette theatre itself is a kind of kinetic art, with the puppeteer part of the artwork. The pendulum principle operates not only within the puppet itself but also in the interaction between it and the puppet player.

Interaction between player and puppet

The marionette will not always do precisely those movements the player wants it to. One option in this case is to take counter-action, forcing it to do the intended movement. The other is to take the lead from the marionette, follow its movements and bring them into the action. This is often the wiser choice. Unplanned actions of this kind can be a source of great creative potential. They call for intuitive responses by the puppeteer, who comes to see his marionette as a partner with a life of its own and to tolerate a certain degree of autonomy on its part. The result can be a virtuous cycle, with puppeteer and puppet interacting with each other. The figure may even acquire such a level of independence that for brief, happy moments it takes over control from the puppeteer and guides him instead. And if the player has the courage to follow the lead, the result can be wonderful situations he would never have thought of. And he then realizes that he is not the supreme controller; rather, it is he who serves the figure. He breathes life into the marionette. He becomes part of it, with all his senses, and feels and experiences what the figure seems to feel and experience. And it is not always clear who is controlling whom.

Marlene Gmelin und Detlef Schmelz mit Paulchen und Pauline

Marlene Gmelin and Detlef Schmelz with Paul und Pauline

Die Kunst des Marionettenbaus

Die Gestaltung

Ein Bildhauer hält mit seiner Skulptur einen momentanen Ausdruck fest. All sein Schaffen gilt dieser einen Pose. Beim Bau einer Marionette hingegen steht die Beweglichkeit im Vordergrund. Weil sie in allen möglichen Posen ausdrucksstark sein soll, wird ihre Gestaltung auf das Wesentliche reduziert. Auf den ersten Blick kann sie deshalb sogar simpel wirken. Doch genau diese Schlichtheit zeichnet eine Theaterfigur aus.

Eine gute Marionette ist für die Bewegung und die Wirkung im Licht gemacht. Durch ihre einfach gehaltene Gestaltung kann der Zuschauer sie mit Fantasie füllen. Licht und Schatten, Haltung und Bewegung lassen sie lebendig werden. Obwohl ihre Mimik sich nicht verändert, zeigt eine gute Marionette im Spiel die verschiedensten Gefühle. Sie kann gelassen oder zornig, fröhlich oder traurig wirken.

The art of marionette making

The design

When a sculptor creates a figure, he freezes a momentary pose or expression for all time. All his creativity is focused on this one moment. When making a marionette, by contrast, the focus is on mobility. As the figure should be equally expressive in all possible poses, its design is reduced to the essentials. At first sight, therefore, it may even appear simplistic. But it is precisely this simplicity that marks the character of a theatrical figure.

A good marionette is made for movement and its effect in various lights. Because of the simplicity of its design, the spectators can fill it according to their own fancy. Light and shade, posture and movement bring it to life. Although its facial expression remains unchanged, a good marionette, played well, can display the whole gamut of feelings, appearing at ease or angry, happy or sad.

Ein guter Marionettenkopf zeichnet sich durch klare Linien und Flächen aus, in denen Licht und Schatten wirken können.

A good marionette head is characterized by clear lines and surfaces that allow a play of light and shadow.

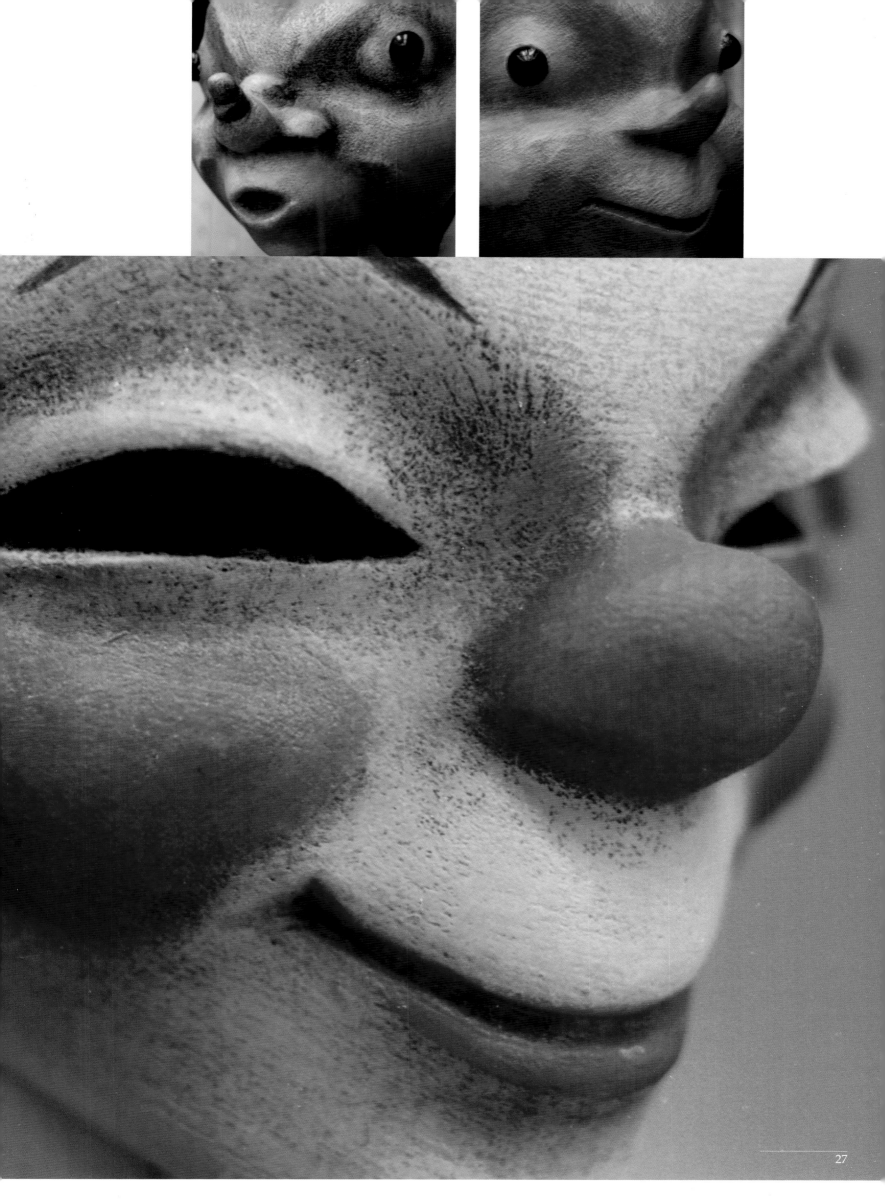

Eine künstle-
risch gestaltete
Marionette ist
eine Skulptur,
die ihre Aussa-
gekraft durch
die ihr eigenen
Bewegungen
wesentlich ver-
stärken kann.

An artfully
made marionette
is a sculpture
that can hugely
amplify its force
of expression
through the in-
dividuality of its
movements.

Die Aufgabe des Marionettenbildners ist es, der Figur ein möglichst weites Spektrum an Ausdrucks- und Bewegungsmöglichkeiten zu geben. Sie kann durchaus so gegensätzliche Gefühle wie Freude und Trauer ausdrücken.

The task of the marionette maker is to give the figure as broad a range of expression and movement as possible. If well made, it can equally well express such opposing feelings as joy and sorrow.

Die Körperschwerpunkte

Schon beim Bau der Marionette leiten – ebenso wie später beim Spiel – die physikalischen Gesetze das Geschehen. Wir haben schon gesehen, dass die Marionette – weil sie an Fäden hängt – zu einem komplexen Pendel wird. Sie besteht aus dem Hauptpendel „Rumpf" mit den Gliedern als Nebenpendeln. Wie bei einem Mobile hängen die Bewegungen der Marionette davon ab, wie die einzelnen Pendel gegeneinander austariert und wie sie miteinander verbunden sind. Für das richtige Zusammenspiel der einzelnen Pendel beschäftigt sich der Marionettenbildner von Anfang an eingehend mit der Anatomie des darzustellenden Körpers. Will er einen Menschen darstellen, so setzt er sich mit der menschlichen Anatomie auseinander, um

> Jede Bewegung, sagte er, hätte einen Schwerpunkt; es wäre genug, diesen, in dem Inneren der Figur, zu regieren; die Glieder, welche nichts als Pendel wären, folgten, ohne irgend ein Zutun, auf eine mechanische Weise von selbst.
>
> Heinrich von Kleist

festzulegen, wo sich die Schwerpunkte befinden und wie die Gelenke beschaffen sind. Auch die Gewichtsverteilung zwischen Rumpf und Gliedern ist von großer Bedeutung. Beim Menschen liegt der Hauptschwerpunkt im Becken. Die Nebenschwerpunkte befinden sich in den Unterarmen, den Oberschenkeln und im Kopf. Für natürlich wirkende Bewegungen platziert der Marionettenbauer ein Bleigewicht in den Beckenbereich. Wenn nötig, tariert er die Figur zusätzlich mit kleineren Gewichten in den Gliedern aus. Weil eine gute Marionette möglichst leicht sein sollte, verbieten sich massive Köpfe aus Holz oder Ton. Kopf und Glieder bestimmen durch ihr Eigengewicht die Schwere des Bleigewichtes im Becken. Marionetten mit wackeligem Gang und drehenden Schultern haben oft einen zu schweren Kopf, der den Schwerpunkt nach oben verlagert. Liegt der Schwerpunkt zu tief, wirkt der Gang schwerfällig.

The centres of gravity

The construction of a marionette – as also later on, when it is being played – is guided by the laws of physics. As we have already seen, a marionette – being suspended on strings – is a form of complex pendulum. It consists of the trunk of the body, as the principal pendulum, and the limbs as additional pendulums. As with a mobile, the movements of a marionette depend on how the individual pendulums are connected with and counterbalance each other. To ensure that the individual pendulums all interact properly, one of the first steps of the marionette maker is to examine the anatomy of the figure he is making in close detail. If he is representing a human figure, he will study the human anatomy in order to determine the location of the centres of gravity and the nature of the various joints. The weight distribution between the trunk and the limbs is another highly important factor. In humans, the main centre of gravity is located in the region of the pelvis. Subsidiary centres of gravity are to be found in the lower arms, the thighs and the head. To achieve movements that appear natural, the marionette maker places a lead weight in the pelvic region. If necessary, he will additionally balance out the figure with smaller weights in the limbs. As a good marionette should be as light as possible, heads made of solid wood or clay are ruled out. The weight of the head and limbs determines how heavy the lead weight in the pelvis needs to be. If a marionette has a

> Every movement, he said, had a centre of gravity; it would be sufficient to position this within the body of the figure; the limbs which were nothing but pendulums, followed mechanically by their own accord, without the puppet-master having to do anything else.
>
> Heinrich von Kleist

wobbly gait and twisting shoulders, the reason in many cases is that the head is too heavy, causing the centre of gravity to be too high. If the centre of gravity is too low, on the other hand, the gait appears heavy and ponderous.

Die Lage des Schwerpunktes bestimmt die Bewegungscharakteristik der Figur. Hier beim Fuchs - eigentlich ein Vierfüßler - liegt er etwa am Ansatz des Brustkorbes. Beim Hasen dagegen liegt der Schwerpunkt im Becken.

The location of the centre of gravity determines the movement characteristics of a figure. In four-legged animals, like the fox shown here, it is located around the start of the rib cage. In a rabbit, on the other hand, it is in the pelvis.

Die Gelenke

Auch für den Bau der Gelenke ist es wesentlich, sich eingehend mit der Anatomie zu beschäftigen. Gelenk für Gelenk ist auf Funktion und Bewegungsumfang zu untersuchen. Der Marionettenbildner muss genau verstanden haben, wie das jeweilige Gelenk funktioniert. Dieses kann er dann mit sehr ausgereiften oder mit einfachsten Mitteln umsetzen. In beiden Fällen kann eine gute Marionette entstehen. Das menschliche Kniegelenk beispielsweise ist ein Scharniergelenk mit einem Bewegungsumfang von knapp 180 Grad. Deshalb wird das Kniegelenk der Marionette als Klappgelenk mit einer Begrenzung von knapp 180 Grad gebaut. Wesentlich ist auch, dass es wie jedes andere Marionettengelenk präzise, leise und zuverlässig funktioniert. Um dies zu erreichen, sind die Kniegelenke von Pendel-Marionetten in der Regel aus Metall. Dazu ist in das Ende des Oberschenkels, welches das Knie bildet, ein Führungsschlitz eingearbeitet. Durch die beiden Schenkel neben diesem Führungsschlitz ist lateral ein Stift eingelassen. Um diesen Stift dreht sich das Ende des Unterschenkels.
Wie wichtig die Begrenzung des Bewegungsumfangs ist, sieht man gut am Halsgelenk. Mit einem nicht begrenzten Kugelgelenk könnte der Kopf nach hinten wegdrehen, was beim Spiel leicht passieren kann. Als einfachste Lösung bietet sich hier eine Öse mit durchgezogener Schnur an. Eleganter und präziser, allerdings aufwendiger ist ein reines Schnurgelenk. Ein Hüftgelenk, bei dem sich die Beine sowohl nach vorn und hinten als auch – bis zu einem gewissen Grad – zur Seite bewegen, sorgt für einen anmutigen Gang. Zudem erlaubt es der Marionette, die beim Theaterspiel so wichtigen Rückwärtsschritte zu gehen. Weil im Becken der Hauptschwerpunkt liegt, spielt das Hüftgelenk auch für die Gesamtbewegung eine bedeutende Rolle. Es lässt sich aus Schnur, Leder oder gebogenem Draht fertigen. Die Pendel-Marionetten sind mit einem Kugelgelenk mit seitlichem Schlitz im Oberschenkel ausgestattet, was Kugel und Pfanne im menschlichen Hüftgelenk entspricht.

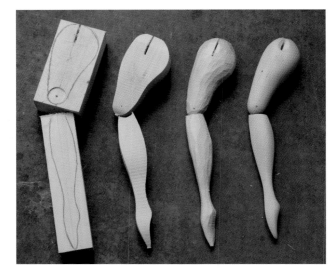

The joints

Also for the construction of the joints, it is necessary to look closely at real-life anatomy. The mode of function and scope of movement of each joint must be studied carefully. The marionette maker must understand exactly how each particular joint works. He can then reproduce this, employing either highly sophisticated or the simplest of means. In either case, the result can be a good marionette. The human knee, for example, is a hinge joint with a range of movement bordering on 180 degrees. The knee joint of a marionette is therefore constructed as a folding joint with movement restricted to around 180 degrees. Another essential requirement is that the knee, like all the other joints of a marionette, should function precisely, reliably and noiselessly. To achieve this, the knee joints of pendulum marionettes are usually made of metal. For this purpose, a slot is cut in the lower end of the thigh segment, and a cross pin is inserted through the two protrusions that form the sides of the slot. The top end of the lower leg section then turns around this pin.
How important it is to restrict the range of movement can be seen by the neck joint. With an unrestricted ball joint, the head could tip backwards – something that can easily happen during performance. The easiest solution to this problem is to fit an eyelet with a thread drawn through it. A more precise and elegant solution, though more complicated to make, is a full string joint. A hip joint that allows the legs to move not only forwards and backwards, but to

Alle Bohrungen und Fräsungen werden gemacht, solange das Werkstück rechtwinklig is. Erst wenn die beiden Teile des Gelenks exakt aneinander angepasst sind, kann die übrige Ausgestaltung der Glieder erfolgen.

All drilling and milling must be done while the workpiece is still rectangular. Only when the two parts that make up a joint are an exact match can the other shaping and finishing work of the limbs be done.

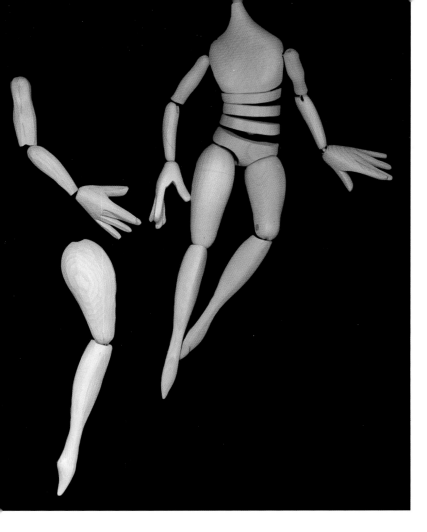

Wenn alle Gelenke ihrem anatomischen Vorbild nach funktionieren, kann die Marionette nur natürliche Haltungen annehmen.

Provided all the joints work as they do in real life, a marionette cannot help having natural posture and movements.

Bei bekleideten Figuren spielt es eine untergeordnete Rolle, wie die Gelenke aussehen. Hingegen sind sichtbare Gelenke eine Herausforderung an den Marionettenbildner. In jeder Bewegung und in jeder Position, welche die Marionette einnehmen kann, sollen die beiden Gelenkschenkel harmonisch zueinander passen und fließend ineinander übergehen. Die Gliederketten, z. B. Oberarm, Unterarm und Hand, sind deshalb als Ganzes zu betrachten.

Präzise Gelenke lassen sich nur herstellen, solange das Werkstück rechtwinklig ist. Denn nur dann kann exakt gesägt, gebohrt und gefräst werden. Weil die Marionette aus vielen Einzelteilen besteht, ist eine gute Planung des Baus notwendig. Das ist ein spannender Prozess, bei dem sich erst ganz am Schluss zeigt, ob die Marionette in allen Bewegungen überzeugt. Erst wenn alle Gelenke sich wie geplant bewegen lassen, kann die Ausgestaltung der Körperteile erfolgen.

Vom Wissen und der Sorgfalt des Marionettenbildners hängt es ab, wie er die physikalischen Anforderungen in der Marionette umsetzt. Wenn er die genannten Punkte beachtet, werden die Bewegungen der Marionette völlig natürlich erscheinen. Groteske, unnatürliche Bewegungen können dann gar nicht erst entstehen.

some degree also sideways, produces a graceful gait. It also allows the marionette to take backward steps – an ability which is important in theatre performance. As the principal centre of gravity is located in the pelvic region, the hip joint plays an important role for the movement altogether. It can be made from string, leather or bent wire. Pendulum Pendel marionettes are equipped with a ball joint with a slot in the side at the top of the thigh segment, corresponding to the ball and socket of the human hip joint.

In the case of clothed figures, it is of only minor importance what the joints look like. Visible joints, however, are a challenge for the marionette maker. In every movement and every posture which the marionette is able to adopt, the two segments that meet at the joint should form a smooth match, both physically and visually. The series of segments that make up a limb, e.g. upper arm, forearm and hand, must therefore be seen as a whole.

Precise joints can only be created as long as the workpiece is rectangular. For only in that state is it possible to saw, drill or mill with precision. A marionette consists of many individual components; therefore, careful planning of construction is essential. That is a suspenseful process, as it only emerges right at the end whether all the marionette's movements are convincing. Only if and when all the joints have been found to move as planned should the further finishing work be done on the parts concerned.

How the physical requirements are actually implemented within the marionette depends on the knowledge and care of the marionette maker. Provided he observes the points outlined above, the marionette's movements will appear completely natural, and all possibility of grotesque, unnatural movements will be ruled out.

Das Spielkreuz und die Fäden

Im Spielkreuz laufen alle Fäden zusammen, von hier aus werden alle Funktionen gesteuert. Dafür gibt es ganz unterschiedliche Methoden. In manchen Kulturen laufen alle Fäden durch einen Ring, und der Spieler legt sich die einzelnen Fäden gekonnt und kunstvoll über Finger, Handrücken und Arme. Dieses Spiel wirkt geradezu artistisch und bedarf langer Übung. Auch beim T-förmigen Spielkreuz, das in unserem Kulturkreis sehr gebräuchlich ist, müssen viele Fäden einzeln gezogen werden.

Anzustreben ist ein in sich flexibles Spielkreuz, das sich intuitiv einfach führen lässt und zudem gut in der Hand liegt.

An diesem hängt die Marionette ausgewogen wie ein Mobile und bedarf nur einer geringen Animation, um sich komplex zu bewegen. Wie bei einem Musikinstrument lernt der Spieler die einzelnen Handgriffe, er lernt diese zu kombinieren und harmonisch zu verbinden. Wenn das Spielkreuz funktionell konstruiert ist, erwecken kleine Finger- und Handbewegungen des Spielers komplexe Bewegungen der Marionette. Da die Fäden senkrecht laufen, gibt die Figur die Maße des Spielkreuzes vor. So ergibt sich beispielsweise die Breite des Kopfholzes aus der Breite des Marionettenkopfes. Das Gleiche gilt für die anderen Spielkreuzteile, sodass man mit etwas Fantasie die Figur im Spielkreuz gespiegelt findet. Das Vogelspielkreuz bildet einen Vogel ab und das Menschenspielkreuz eine Person.

Kreuz und Figur sind immer aufeinander abgestimmt. Grundsätzlich sollte eine Marionette nur an so vielen Fäden hängen wie notwendig. Weniger ist – auch hier – mehr. Doch diese wenigen Fäden müssen „sitzen". Der Marionettenbildner sucht oft stundenlang in konzentrierter Arbeit, bis er die idealen Anknüpfpunkte gefunden hat. Wenn sowohl die Figur als auch das Spielkreuz optimal konstruiert sind, wird die Marionette im Spiel überzeugen.

The control bar and strings

All the strings are attached to the control bar, and it is from here that all the functions are steered. There are different ways this can be done. In some cultures, all the strings run through a ring and the player lays the individual strings artfully over the fingers, backs of the haTnds and arms. This method of playing appears nothing short of artistic and requires very much practice.

Also with the T-shaped control bar, which is commonly used in our part of the world, a large number of strings have to be individually manipulated. The aim should be for a flexible control bar that can be handled easily and intuitively and lies comfortably in the hand.

The marionette is suspended from this – in a state of balance, like a mobile – and requires only little animation in order to perform complex movements. As with a musical instrument, the player learns the various handholds and how to combine them to achieve a harmonious result.

However, the foundation for this must be laid in advance by the marionette maker. If he has created an optimally functioning control bar, only small hand and finger movements of the player are sufficient to generate complex movements by the marionette. As the strings all fall vertically, the figure is mirrored in the control bar. The breadth of the head plate, for example, mirrors the breadth of the marionette's head. The same also applies to the other sections of the control bar, so that with a little imagination, the figure can be seen reflected in the control bar. A bird control bar emulates a bird, a human control bar a person. The control bar and figure are always matched to one another. As a general rule, a marionette should only be suspended on as many strings as necessary. This is

Die Fäden verbinden nicht nur, sie trennen auch! Sie schaffen eine Distanz zwischen Spieler und Figur. Keine andere Führungstechnik lässt der Figur so viel Freiheit, ein Eigenleben zu entfalten wie die der Marionette.
Da ihr Schwerpunkt in ihrem Innern liegt, scheint sie allein aus sich heraus zu agieren. Sie ist auf der Bühne präsent, kann laufen, springen, tanzen und ist dabei optisch weitgehend vom Spieler gelöst. Selbst wenn der Betrachter den Marionettenspieler wahrnimmt, glaubt er aufgrund ihrer feinen Gesten und ihrer differenzierten Körperhaltungen ein eigenständiges Wesen vor sich zu haben.

yet another instance of less being more. However, those few strings must all be perfectly placed. It may take the marionette maker hours of concentrated work to find the ideal connection points. If both the figure itself and the control bar are optimally designed and made, the marionette will perform convincingly.

Das Wechselspiel zwischen Marionette, Spieler und Betrachter

Marionette und Spieler

Ein geschickter Spieler kann, weil er die Pendelgesetze kennt und in sein Spiel integriert, die Marionette so führen, dass ihr nicht nur der Bühnenboden gehört, sondern auch die Luft darüber. Die Marionette läuft nicht wirklich auf der Erde, sondern deutet in ihren Bewegungen nur an, dass sie auf ihr geht. Sie könnte auch in der Luft gehen oder stehen. Den Boden braucht sie nur, um die Schwerkraft darzustellen. Dann assoziiert der Zuschauer, dass sie real geht, steht oder handelt. Die Überwindung der Schwerkraft, die Leichtigkeit, das schwerelose Dahingleiten – diese Elemente des Tanzes sind für die Marionette mühelos zu verwirklichen. Mit ihnen kann im Wechselspiel zwischen Boden und Luft der überirdisch schöne Tanz gelingen, zu dem der Balletttänzer in Kleists Aufsatz „Über das Marionettentheater" selbst nicht in der Lage ist. Doch die Marionette voll-

> Die Marionette erscheint beseelt,
> verleugnet dabei aber keinen Moment,
> dass sie eine künstliche Figur ist.
>
> Marcel Marceau

bringt das nicht allein. Sie braucht dazu einen Marionettenspieler, für den das Tanzen zum Leben gehört. Im virtuosen Tanz der Marionette werden deshalb beide – Spieler und Marionette – tanzen. Mal wird der eine und mal der andere führen.

The interaction between the marionette, player and spectator

The marionette and the player

A skilful player – one who is familiar with the laws governing the motion of pendulums and utilizes them in his performance – can handle the marionette in such a way that its realm is not only the ground, but also the air above. Naturally, the marionette does not really walk on the ground, but merely suggests by its movements that it is doing so. It could equally well stand or walk in the air. It needs the ground

> The marionette appears animate,
> without denying for one moment
> that it is an artificial figure.
>
> Marcel Marceau

only to represent gravity. And in this case, by association, the viewer believes that it really is standing, walking, or performing some other action. Overcoming gravity, creating the impression of lightness and the ability to float weightlessly – these are elements of dance which a marionette can achieve with ease. Alternating between the ground and the air, a marionette is able to attain that transcendental beauty of movement that is beyond the reach of the real-life ballet dancer in Kleist's essay "Über das Marionettentheater" ("On Marionette Theatre"). However, the marionette is not able to achieve it by itself. To do so, it needs a marionette player for whom dance is part of life. In the virtuoso dance of the marionette, therefore, both player and marionette will dance – with sometimes one taking the lead, and sometimes the other.

Spieler und Betrachter

Nach einem gelungenen Marionettenspiel ist der Blick vieler Zuschauer nach innen gekehrt. Da verwundert es nicht, dass die Pupille, die das Fenster zu unserem Innern darstellt, etymologisch von Pupilla, der Puppe, abstammt. Vordergründig betrachtet, spiegelt sich der Mensch in der Pupille seines Gegenübers als kleines Wesen, als „Puppe". Doch in der Pupille des anderen spiegeln wir uns nicht nur, sondern wir blicken auch in ihn hinein. Wir erkennen, was er empfindet, wie wahrhaftig er ist.

In der Pupille trifft sich das Ich mit dem Du. Ähnlich verhält es sich mit der Pupilla, der Marionette. Eine Marionette ist dann überzeugend gespielt, wenn der Spieler mit all seinen Sinnen in ihr ist und ihr Leben einhaucht. Er durchlebt das, was die Marionette spielt, und sieht die Welt mit ihren Augen. Dem Zuschauer erscheint sie deshalb lebendig. Auch er fühlt und erlebt das, was die Figur vorgibt zu erleben.

So begegnen sich in der Marionette Spieler und Betrachter.

The player and the spectator

At the end of a successful marionette performance, the view of many spectators is turned inwards. Which is perhaps not surprising as pupil – the window to our soul – derives etymologically from the word pupilla, meaning little girl or doll and hence also puppet. Viewed superficially, a person sees himself reflected in miniature, as a "puppet", in the pupil of the person he is speaking to. However, we not only see our reflection in the other person's pupil, we also look through it into that person. We see what he feels, how truthful he is. In the pupil, the "I" and the "you" come together. And something similar happens with the pupilla, the marionette. A marionette performs convincingly when the player imbues it with all his senses and breathes life into it. He experiences what the marionette is playing and sees the world through its eyes. To the spectator, therefore, the marionette appears alive. He, too, feels and experiences what the figure pretends to experience. In this way, the player and spectator meet in the marionette.

Marionette und Betrachter

Der Zuschauer taucht in die Welt der Marionette ein. Er spiegelt sich in der Pupilla, in der sich der Spieler widerspiegelt.

Gleichzeitig weiß er genau, dass die Marionette künstlich ist, dass es nur ein Spiel mit der Fantasie ist. Deshalb lässt er sie bereitwillig viel näher an sich heran, als er es dem Spieler als realer Person jemals erlauben würde. Er schaut auf die Marionette und blickt gleichzeitig in sich hinein. Er bekommt Kontakt zu dem kleinen Menschen in sich, zu seinem inneren Kind.

Marionette, Spieler und Betrachter

Die Marionette übt eine starke Wirkung auf Menschen jedes Alters aus. Sehr subtil berührt sie viel tiefere Schichten als nur die Verstandesebene und wirkt deshalb nachhaltig. Sie wendet sich an das Kind im Menschen – egal wie alt dieser ist. Mit ihr lassen sich Dinge sagen, die von Mensch zu Mensch zu intim wären. Dank der Fäden ist sie ein Wesen der Luft. Diese bleiben dem Betrachter präsent und lassen ihn an ein Zusammenspiel von oben und unten denken, an eine Verstrickung in scheinbar Unabänderliches oder an höhere göttliche Kräfte. Marionettenspiel hat eine archetypische Kraft. Es ist die Kraft und die Magie der „kleinen Marie".

Ich glaube an die unsterbliche Seele
der Marionetten und Puppen ...
es ist etwas Göttliches in ihnen,
wie klein sie auch immer sein mögen.
Sie leben nicht wie unsereiner –
und doch leben sie.

Anatole France

The marionette and the spectator

The spectator becomes immersed in the world of the marionette, and finds himself mirrored in the pupilla in which the player is also reflected. At the same time, he is perfectly aware that the marionette is an artificial figure, that it is all just a play of the imagination. Therefore, he readily allows it to get much closer to him than he would ever allow the player to do as a real person. He sees the marionette, but at the same time looks into himself. He makes contact with the little person inside himself, his inner child.

I believe in the immortal soul
of marionettes and puppets...
There is something divine in them,
however small they may be.
They may not live as we do –
but alive they surely are.

Anatole France

The marionette, player and spectator

A marionette has a powerful effect on people of all ages. It very subtly touches into strata which are much deeper than the conscious mind and so makes a sustained impact on us. It addresses the child in us – however old we may be. It enables things to be said which would be too intimate if spoken from person to person. Thanks to the strings, it is a being of the air. The spectator remains aware of the strings, arousing ideas of interactions between the up and down, of enmeshment in seemingly inexorable events, or the intervention of superior, divine powers. Marionette theatre has an archetypical force. It is the force and magic exercised by "Little Mary".

Das Planen, Entwerfen, Gestalten von Pendel-Marionetten

Planning, designing, construction of Pendel-Marionettes

Unsere Marionetten verkörpern Gestalten aus dem Märchenreich, der Mythologie oder aus fantastischen Welten. Einige sind Einzelfiguren, manche bilden einen Themenkomplex, andere sind das Spielensemble eines Stücks oder Märchens. In der Welt des Theaters ist es wichtig, auch auf größere Entfernung jeden Akteur sofort wiederzuerkennen, sodass „der Gute" nicht mit „dem Bösen" verwechselt werden kann. Schauspieler benutzen deswegen verschiedenartige und -farbige Kostüme und einen spezifischen Bewegungsduktus. Der Schauspieler verkleidet sich und schlüpft in die zu spielende Rolle hinein. Doch kann er seinen Körper nur bedingt verändern. Soll er ein Tier spielen, sieht der Zuschauer sofort, dass nur ein verkleideter Mensch dahintersteckt. Für das Figurentheater wird das Tier in seiner spezifischen Art geformt und gebaut. Seine Bewegungscharakteristik entspricht der jeweiligen Art: Ein Vogel hüpft, breitet die Flügel aus und erhebt sich in die Lüfte. Und gerade das Letztere wäre dem Schauspieler nur mit großem Aufwand möglich. Marionetten sind kein verkleinertes Abbild des Menschen oder des kostümierten Schauspielers, sondern sie werden nach den theatralischen Erfordernissen als eigenständige Wesen speziell für ihre Rolle gestaltet. In der Commedia dell'Arte setzen die Schauspieler Masken auf, um die darzustellende Figur zu verkörpern. Im Figurentheater schnitzt oder formt man den Kopf schon als diesen Charakter aus.

Die Sprache der Marionetten ist die Sprache der Gebärden: Im Spiel drücken sich die Figuren durch gezielte Kopf- und Handbewegungen und entsprechende Körperhaltungen aus. Also wird dem Kopf und den Händen als Hauptausdrucksmittel auch in ihren Größen eine besondere Bedeutung zugemessen. Beim Idealmenschen beträgt das Verhältnis von Kopf zu Körper 1:7. Wir verschieben dieses Verhältnis zugunsten des Kopfes auf 1:5 bis sogar 1:1. Die Größe der Hände richtet sich jedoch nach der Größe des Kopfes: Legt man die Hand mit

Our puppets embody figures from the realms of fairy tales, mythology or from fantastic worlds. Some are individual figures, some form a complex of topics, others a part of a play or fairy tale. In the world of the theatre it is important to be able to recognise every actor immediately from a distance, so that the „Goodie" isn't confused with the „Baddie". Therefore actors wear costumes of different types and colours and have a specific mode of movement. The actor disguises himself and slips into the role to be played. But he can only change his body within given limits. If he is to play an animal, the audience realises immediately that it is only being played by a person in disguise. In the figure theatre, the animal is shaped and constructed in accordance with its specific nature. Its characteristics conform to those of the animal represented. A bird hops, spreads its wings and lifts itself up into the air. And it is precisely the latter which would only be accomplished by the actor with great effort. Marionettes are not a scaled-down image of people or of actors in costume, but are designed specially for their role as an independent beings and to satisfy theatrical requirements. In commedia dell'arte the actors put on masks in order to embody the figure to be represented. In the figure theatre the head is indeed carved or formed to represent this character.

The language of puppets is the language of gesture. In the play the figures express themselves with selected movements of the head and hands and corresponding body posture. Therefore the head and hands are attributed particular significance as the main means of expression, also in terms of their size. In the perfectly formed person the ratio of head to body is 1:7. We adjust this ratio in favour of the head to 1:5 or even as much as 1:1. The size of the hands is however determined by the size of the head. If the hand is placed with the ball of the thumb against the chin, the finger tips should reach to the middle of the forehead. Whereas the hands are capable of making a theatrical statement, the feet are attributed only minor importance.

Die schöne Nymphe Syrinx flieht vor den Nachstellungen des bocksbeinigen Pan. In höchster Not lässt sie sich in Schilfrohr verwandeln. Um trotzdem mit ihr vereinigt zu sein, schneidet Pan das Schilfrohr in unterschiedlich lange Teile, bindet sie zusammen und klagt auf diesem Instrument sein Leid über die verlorene Syrinx.

Syrinx, a beautiful nymph, flees from the advances of goat-legged Pan. In dire distress, she causes herself to be transformed into a reed. To be united with her all the same, Pan cuts the reed into sections of different length, binds them together and plays on the resulting pipes, lamenting his sorrow over the loss of Syrinx.

dem Ansatz des Daumenballens an das Kinn, erreicht man mit den Fingerspitzen die Mitte der Stirn.

Während die Hände eine theatralische Aussage haben, kommt den Füßen nur eine geringe Bedeutung zu. Großes Schuhwerk oder auch schon als normal groß empfundene Füße behindern aufgrund ihrer Form die Fortbewegung erheblich, deshalb verkleinern wir sie zugunsten der Spielfunktion.

Bei der Gestaltung des Gesichts betonen wir das Figurenhafte durch die Verwendung von Perlen als Augen oder durch schwarze Augenschlitze. Letztere verändern bei der Bewegung des Kopfes ihre Form. So „schließt" die Marionette die Augen, wenn der Kopf gesenkt wird. Durch Höhen und Tiefen oder Kanten entstehen im Gesicht Schattenwirkungen, die den Zuschauer glauben lassen, Gefühlsregungen wahrzunehmen. Bei der Planung einer Figur sind sowohl der technische als auch der künstlerische Aspekt zu beachten: Der technische Plan zeigt die Proportionen auf, die Größe der Glieder und die Gelenkverbindungen. Der künstlerische Entwurf skizziert die Form- und Farbgebung.

Bevor wir nun mit Zeichnungen beginnen, entwerfen wir ein Bild von Charakter, Umfeld und Geschichte der Figur, ein „Psycho- und Soziogramm". In welcher Epoche spielt die Handlung? Welcher gesellschaftlichen Schicht gehört die darzustellende Person an?

Large shoes or even large feet which are considered large by normal standards impede walking or running considerably in favour of the function of the puppet for the performance. When designing the face we emphasise the figure by using pearls for eyes or black eye lids. The latter change shape when the head moves. So the puppet „closes" its eyes if the head is lowered. Shadow-like effects are created in the face with raised sections, recesses, or edges which make the onlooker think that he can observe emotions. When designing a figure, not only the technical but also the artistic aspects are to be observed. Technical design illustrates proportions, the size of the limbs, and articulations. The artistic draft sketches styling and colouring.

Before we now begin with diagrams, we design the character an image, inventing the background and history of the figure, a „psycho- and sociogram". In which era does the action take place? Which social class does the person to be represented belong to? In which surroundings does it live? Is it poor or rich? Are its circumstances stable or are they subject to change? Additional questions about the person include age, sex, marital status and health. Is it satisfulfil the intended role? Is it satisfied with itself and its life or is it striving for change? Which outstanding features are characteristic for them? Does it tend to be spiritual characte-

Im Marionettentheater ist alles möglich, denn die Figur wird extra für ihre Rolle entworfen und gebaut. Die Naturgesetze sind aufgehoben.

In marionette theatre, anything is possible since the figures are designed and made specially for their roles and the laws of nature do not apply.

In welchem Umfeld lebt sie? Ist sie arm oder reich? Ist ihre Position stabil oder Veränderungen unterworfen? Weitere Fragen zur Person beinhalten Alter, Geschlecht, Familienstand und Gesundheit. Ist sie mit sich und ihrem Leben zufrieden oder strebt sie nach Veränderung? Welche herausragenden Eigenschaften sind für sie charakteristisch? Gehören zur Erfüllung der vorgesehenen Rolle eher geistige Fähigkeiten, gesunder Menschenverstand, musische Kräfte oder einfach ein starker Wille? Von welchem Temperament wird die Figur beherrscht?

Anhand des Grimm'schen Märchens „Das tapfere Schneiderlein" zeigen wir die Umsetzung der theoretischen Überlegungen in die Praxis.

Zur Person des Schneiderleins:
Es ist männlich, ungefähr 20 Jahre alt, ledig und lebt als Handwerker selbstständig in einem kleinen Städtchen. Seine Verhältnisse sind ärmlich, aber nicht bettelarm. Als Schneider ist er adrett und ordentlich gekleidet. Wir geben ihm folgende persönliche Eigenschaften: Er ist frech, unerschrocken, selbstbewusst und reaktionsschnell. Er verfügt über einen weitblickenden, gesunden Menschenverstand, sodass er die Reaktionen seiner Kontrahenten zu seinem Vorteil nutzen kann.

Dem Schneiderlein ordnen wir natürlich das sanguinische Temperament mit cholerischem Einschlag zu. Seine Geistes- und Willenskräfte sind stärker ausgebildet als sein Gefühlsleben. Als neugieriger, reaktionsschneller Person geben wir ihm offene Augen, eine frech nach oben gebogene Nase und einen optimistischen Mund. Er bekommt blonde Haare und eine schlanke, wendige Gestalt. Die Beine betonen wir durch ihre Länge. Er muss besonders viel laufen und springen, um die ihm gestellten Aufgaben zu lösen. Deshalb ziehen wir ihm auch bequeme Hosen, wie Kniebundhosen, an. Ein Jackett mit fliegenden Schößen unterstreicht seine Leichtigkeit oder auch seinen Leichtsinn. Und der Gürtel darf natürlich nicht vergessen werden.

ristics, common sense, musical talents or simply a strong will which are needed to fulfill the intended role?

Which temperament does the figure possess? Based on the Grimm's fairy tale „The Brave Little Tailor" we show how theoretical considerations are put into practice.

About the character of the little tailor:
He is male, about 20 years old, single, and makes his living as an independent craftsman in a small town. He lives in needy circumstances, but he is not so poor that he has to beg. As a tailor he is smartly and properly dressed. We are going to give him the following personal characteristics: He is impertinent, undaunted, self-conscious and quick to react. He has a farsighted and keen mind, so that he can take the reactions of his adversaries into account to his advantage.

Of course we shall attribute the sanguinary humour with streak of the choleric to the little tailor. His spiritual powers and will power are more strongly developed than his emotional life. As a curious person quick co react, we shall give him open eyes, a cheeky, upturned nose and an optimistic mouth. He is to have blond hair and a slim, agile body. We shall emphasise the legs by their length. He has to run and jump a great deal in order to fulfil the tasks allotted to him. Therefore we shall dress him in comfortable knee-length breeches for trousers. A jacket with flying coat-tails emphasises his grace or even his recklessness. And of course, his belt must not be forgotten.

Blattlaus
Aphis sp.
Familie: Läuse
Größe: bis 7 mm
Lebensraum:
Kultur- und Wildpflanzen

Greenfly
Aphis sp.
Family: Lice
Size: up to 7 mm
Habitat:
Cultivated and wild plants

Gemeine Stechmücke
Culex pipiens
Familie: Zweiflügler
Größe: 3,5 bis 5 mm
Lebensraum:
Stehende Gewässer

Ordinary Mosqitto
Culex pipiens
Family: Diptera
Size: 3,5 to 5 mm
Habitat:
Standing waters

Heideschnecke
Hellicella obvia
Familie: Schnirkelschnecken
Größe: Gehäuse 8 x 16 mm
Lebensraum: Waldlose Hänge
und Bahndämme

Heath Snail
Hellicella obvia
Family: Helicellidae
Size: Shell 8 x 16 mm
Habitat: Grassy hillsides
and railway embankments

Mehlmotte
Ephestia kuchinella
Familie: Zünsler
Größe: 8 bis 12 mm
Lebensraum: Mühlen,
Bäckereien, Kleiderschränke

Flour Moth
Ephestia kuchinella
Family: Pyralidae
Size: 8 to 12 mm
Habitat:
Mills, bakeries, wardrobes

ierpunkt
dalia quatripunctata
amilie: Marienkäfer
röße: 3,5 bis 5,5 mm
ebensraum: Überwintern oft
 menschlichen Behausungen

Four-Spot
Adalia quatripunctata
Family: Ladybirds
Size: 3,5 to 5,5 mm
Habitat: Overwinter often in
human habitations

Grünes Heupferd
Terrigonia viridissima
Familie: Singschrecken
Größe: 28 bis 42 mm
Lebensraum: Sträucher,
Feld - und Wiesenpflanzen

Great green Bush-Cricket
Terrigonia viridissima
Family: Orthoptera
Size: 28 to 42 mm
Habitat: Shrubs,
field and meadow plants

Gottesanbeterin
Mantis religiosa
amilie: Fangschrecken
Größe: 40 bis 75 mm
ebensraum: Trockenwarme
iotope, Südhäng

Praying Mantis
Mantis religiosa
Family: Mantidae
Size: 40 to 75 mm
Habitat: Dry-warm biotops,
southern mountain slopes

Ampferfeuerfalter
Heodes hippothoé
Familie: Falter
Größe: 30 bis 36 mm
Lebensraum:
Feuchtwiesen

Purble-edged Copper
Heodes hippothoé
Family: Butterflies
Size: 30 to 36 mm
Habitat:
Damp meadows

Aus der Pendel-Werkstatt

Nachdem die formale Gestalt der Marionette ergründet wurde, wenden wir uns nun den technischen Aspekten zu. Am Beispiel einer Katze möchten wir unsere Arbeitsweise als Marionettenbildner darstellen.

Als Erstes stellt sich immer die Frage nach der Lage des Schwerpunktes im Körper. Wie bereits zuvor beschrieben, wird die gesamte Bewegungscharakteristik der Marionette durch dessen Position bestimmt, denn jede Bewegung ist abhängig von ihrem Schwerpunkt. Während der Mensch als Zweifüßler den Schwerpunkt ziemlich genau im Becken hat, befindet sich dieser beim Vierfüßler zwischen Vorder- und Hinterbeinen etwa am Ansatz des Brustkorbes. Das bedeutet nicht zwangsläufig, dass man genau dort ein Gewicht platzieren muss, denn das Material, aus dem der Körper geformt wird, hat ja auch ein Eigengewicht.

In Vielem ähnelt eine Marionette
einer guten Geige.
Ihre Qualität offenbart sich erst im Spiel.
Ihr Bau bedarf Können,
Sorgfalt und Wissen.

Detlef Schmelz

Es geht nur darum, dass durch die Gewichtsverteilung im Körper der Gesamtschwerpunkt dorthin gelangt. Es sollte immer das Ziel sein, die Figur so leicht wie möglich zu bauen, damit man sie auch leicht spielen kann.

Wir beschäftigen uns eingehend mit der Anatomie der Katze. Zwar können wir unmöglich ein Wesen erschaffen, welches alle Bewegungen einer lebenden Katze abbildet, aber wir können ihre wesentlichen Bewegungsabläufe herausarbeiten und versuchen, diese möglichst natürlich umzusetzen. Dazu ermitteln wir zunächst die Proportionen der Gliedmaßen und des Körpers und legen fest, auf welche Bewegungsabläufe sie reduziert werden sollte. Für jedes einzelne Gelenk ermitteln wir die Funktion.

From the Pendel workshop

Now that we have looked at the formal design of a marionette, we can turn our attention to the technical aspects. We would like to illustrate how we make a marionette using the example of a cat.

The first question that always needs to be answered is the location of the centre of gravity within the body. As has already been explained, this completely determines the movement characteristics of a marionette, for every movement depends on its centre of gravity.

In many regards, a marionette
is like a good violin.
Its quality only reveals itself when it is played.
Its construction calls for skill,
care and knowledge."

Detlef Schmelz

The centre of gravity of humans, as two-legged beings, is located almost exactly in the pelvis; in four-legged creatures, on the other hand, it lies between the front and back legs, around the start of the rib cage. That does not necessarily mean placing a weight at precisely that point; after all, the material the body is made of also has a weight of its own. All it means is that, given the weight distribution of the body as a whole, the main centre of gravity is located in that position. And the aim should always be to make the figure as light as possible so as to make it easy to play.

So we carefully study the anatomy of a cat. Obviously, we cannot create a figure that is able to imitate all the movements of a real-life cat, but we can identify its main movements and try to recreate these as naturally as possible. To do that, we first establish the proportions of the limbs and body and decide which of the whole range of movements to restrict ourselves to. We then study the mode of operation of each joint.

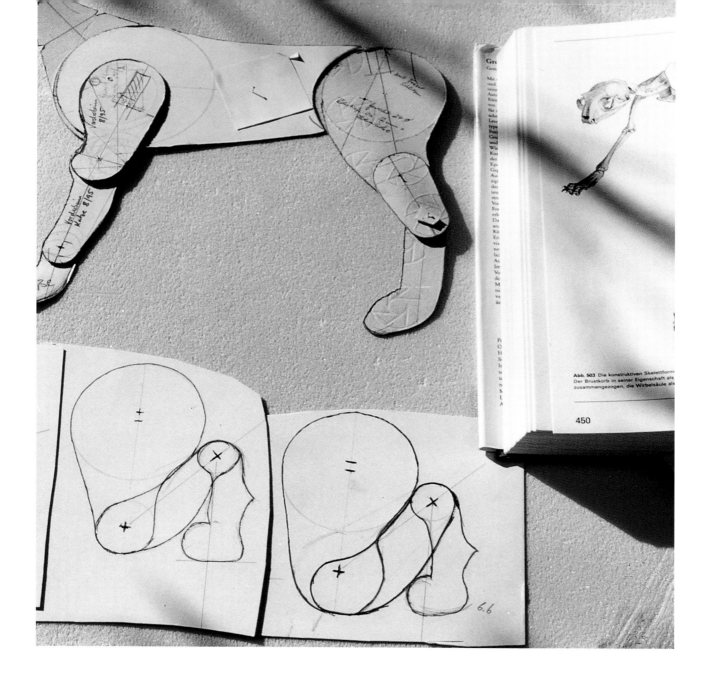

Ist es ein reines Klappgelenk oder ein Klapp-Drehgelenk wie im menschlichen Unterarm? Sodann legen wir den Freiheitsgrad und die Endpunkte der Bewegung fest.

Anhand von anatomischen Zeichnungen fertigen wir Schablonen an und ermitteln so die Funktionen der Gelenke und die mögliche Gestalt der einzelnen Glieder.

Die Figur kann sich gar nicht anders bewegen als auf eine natürliche Art und Weise, wenn wir die Haupt- und Nebenschwerpunkte richtig setzen und die einzelnen Gelenke in ihren Wirkungsgraden so bauen, wie es die Anatomie vorgibt. Deshalb ist es so wichtig, sich über die Bewegungsfreiheiten der einzelnen Gelenke bewusst zu werden. Wie sie in die Praxis umgesetzt werden, ist eher zweitrangig. Ein Stück Schnur kann genauso wirkungsvoll sein wie ein kompliziertes Kardangelenk. Entscheidend ist einzig die Funktion.

Is it a simple hinge joint, or a hinge and swivel joint as in the human forearm? As the next step, we set the range and end points of the movement.

Based on anatomical drawings, we produce templates which we use to establish the functioning of the joints and the possible shape of the individual sections.

Provided we position the main and subsidiary centres of gravity correctly and allow the individual joints with the same range of movement as a real-life animal possesses, the figure cannot help moving in a natural way. That is why it is so important to know the extent of movement of the individual joints. How this outcome is then achieved in practice is of only secondary importance. A piece of string can be just as effective as a complex universal joint. All that matters is the correct function.

Hier werden aus einer gut abgelagerten Lindenbohle Bretter gesägt, die anschließend exakt rechtwinklig gehobelt werden.

Here, boards are being sawn from a well-seasoned piece of lime tree wood; the boards will then be planed to form exact right angles.

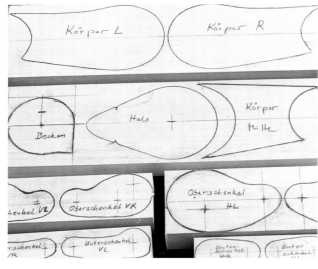

Beim Aufzeichnen der auszusägenden Teile wird genau auf den Maserungsverlauf geachtet.

When marking the parts to be cut out, careful attention is paid to the run of the grain.

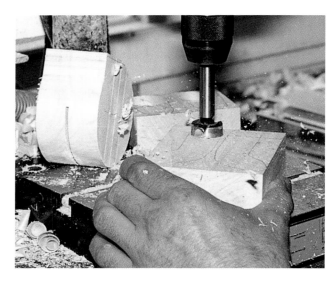

Alle Bohrungen und Fräsungen werden gemacht, solange das Werkstück rechtwinklig ist. Deshalb werden die Gelenkpunkte und Begrenzungen exakt festgelegt und markiert.

All milling and drilling is done while the workpiece is still in its rectangular form. Therefore, the swivel and end points have to be precisely identified and marked.

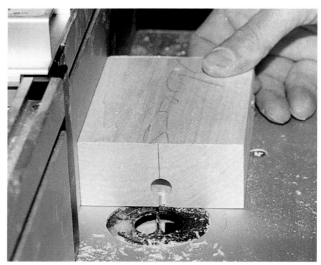

Mit der Fräse werden die Gelenke geschlitzt. Beide Teile eines Gelenkes sollten präzise zueinander passen.

The joints are slotted using a milling machine. This ensures that both sections of a joint are an exact match.

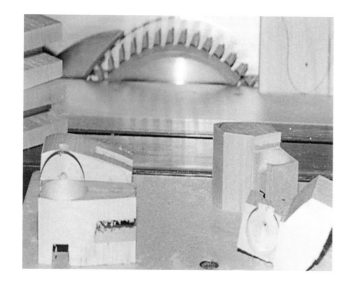

Erst nach diesen Vorarbeiten werden die einzelnen Teile ausgesägt.

Only when all this preliminary work has been completed are the individual pieces actually cut out.

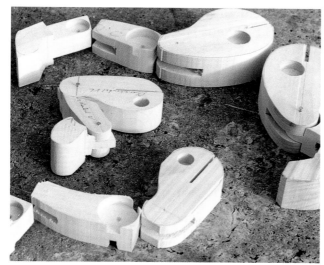

Die Konturen werden mit der Bandschleifmaschine nachgearbeitet und die Gelenke aneinander angepasst.

The contours are finished off using a belt grinding machine and the joints made to fit one another.

Die Schwerpunktgewichte werden aus Blei gegossen. Schon bei der Planung wurden ihre Platzierung und das jeweils benötigte Gewicht ermittelt.

The weights for the centres of gravity are cast from molten lead. The position and weight were already calculated during the planning phase.

Nachdem der Rumpf zusammengeleimt wurde, wird die Figur provisorisch zusammengefügt.

Once the torso has been glued together, the figure is put together on a provisional basis.

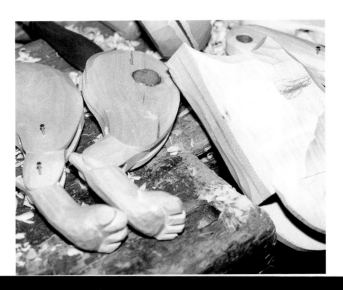

Alle Teile werden nun ge-
schnitzt und immer wieder
aneinander angepasst.

All parts are now cut and fit-
ted together again and again.

Gestaltete Welten

Fascinating scenes

Kopf und Hände sind die Hauptausdrucksmittel der Marionette. Die gekonnte Ausarbeitung des Kopfes bewirkt im Zusammenspiel von Bewegung, Licht und Schatten die Mimik. Die Gestaltung der Hände unterstützt den Charakter der Figur wesentlich.

The head and hands are the main means of expression for a marionette. It is skilful design of the head – in conjunction with movement, light and shade – that generates the facial expressions. The design of the hands contributes hugely to the character of the figure. A well-designed hand brings the play to life.

Das Spiel mit Pendel-Marionetten

Playing with Pendel marionettes

Vor dem eigentlichen Spiel sollte sich der Marionettenspieler über die Konstruktion des Spielkreuzes bewusst werden. Das Pendel-Spielkreuz ist eine Weiterentwicklung des sogenannten Brosskreuzes. Wesentliches Konstruktionsmerkmal sind die stufenlos in alle Richtungen verstellbaren Armausleger, die am Kopfholz befestigt sind. Hand- und Kopfbewegung lassen sich so auf vielfältige Weise miteinander verknüpfen. Durch einfaches Drehen und Wenden des Kreuzes werden, je nach Einstellung der Armausleger, harmonische Bewegungsabläufe möglich. Selten ist es nötig, einzelne Fäden zu ziehen.

Am einfachsten wird die Funktion des Pendel-Spielkreuzes erklärbar, wenn man sich im Spielkreuz oben die Marionette unten nochmals abgebildet vorstellt: In der Schulterschwinge die Schulter, im Gelenk darüber den Hals, im Spielkreuzgriff den Kopf, in den Handhölzern die Hände.

Bevor Sie mit den eigentlichen Spielübungen beginnen, sollten Sie sich der Positionen im Marionettentheater bewusst werden: Der Marionettenspieler steht immer hinter der Figur! Im Querschnitt könnte es so gesagt werden: *Zuschauer – Marionette – Spieler.*

Jede Handlung wird vom Kopf bestimmt und somit durch eine Kopfbewegung eingeleitet.

Für die nun folgenden Spielübungen markieren Sie bitte auf einem kurzflorigen Teppich eine Spielfläche von etwa 2 x 1 Metern. In diesem Bühnenraum lassen Sie die Marionette hin und her schweben. Dabei halten Sie das Spielkreuz so, dass es sich immer seitlich neben Ihrem Becken befindet. Sie selbst bewegen sich also in kleinen Schritten parallel zur Figur. Da Sie immer im Hintergrund bleiben müssen, wird am jeweiligen Bühnenende ein Wechsel der Spielkreuzhand fällig. Diesen kombinieren Sie am besten mit einer Kopf- und Körperdrehung wie bei der nächsten Übung. Verzichten Sie beim Erlernen der Grundübungen unbedingt auf einen Spiegel! Er bringt Sie nur durcheinander. Bitten Sie eine zweite Person, Ihnen widerzuspiegeln, was sie von vorn sieht, und lernen Sie so die Stellungen der Marionette von oben, also aus der Spielerposition, zu beurteilen.

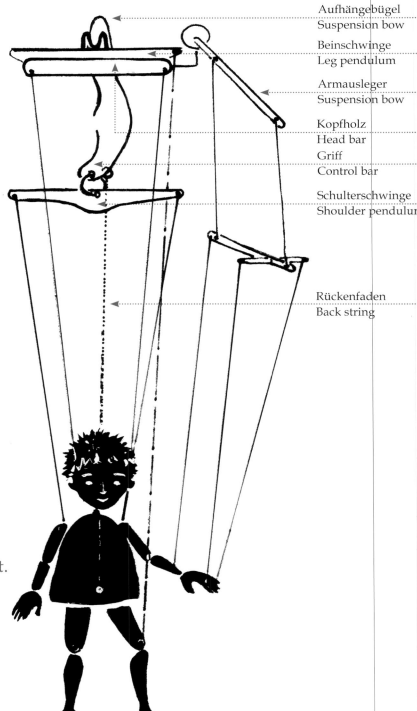

Aufhängebügel
Suspension bow

Beinschwinge
Leg pendulum

Armausleger
Suspension bow

Kopfholz
Head bar

Griff
Control bar

Schulterschwinge
Shoulder pendulum

Rückenfaden
Back string

The Pendel control bar is a further development of the so-called „Bross control bar". Main construction features of both systems are the arm jibs, which are continuously variable in all directions and fixed to the head bar. The movements of hand and head can thus be combined with each other in a varied manner. Depending on the adjustment, very harmonious sequences of movements are possible by

simply turning the bar. It is only rarely necessary to pull individual strings. The easiest way to understand the functioning of the Pendel control bar is to imagine the control bar above to be a reproduction of the puppet below: The shoulder pendulum represents the shoulder, the joint on top of it represents the neck, the control bar handle represents the head, the hand bars represent the hands.

Before starting the actual exercise, you should become aware of the positions in the marionette theatre:

The puppeteer always stands behind the figure! This means that the positions are placed in the following cross-section:
Onlooker – Marionette – Puppeteer.

Before starting with the following exercises, please mark an area of about 2 x 1 m on a short pile carpet. Let the puppet float to and fro within this stage area. Hold the control bar so that it is always at the side next to your pelvis.

Each human action is determined by the mind and thus initiated by a movement of the head.

This means that you have to move in small steps parallel to the figure. As you always have to stay in the background, a change of the control bar hand is necessary every time that you reach the end of the stage. It is recommendable to combine this change of hands with a turn of head or body. When learning the basic exercises, it is absolutely necessary to do without a mirror! This would just confuse you. Ask another person to reflect what he or she sees from a position in front of you and thus learn to judge the movements of the marionette from above.

Für alle, die das Spiel mit der Marionette erlernen möchten, geben Marlene Gmelin und Detlef Schmelz Marionetten-spielkurse.

Marlene Gmelin and Detlef Schmelz offer all those people who would like to learn how to play a puppet both beginners' and advanced courses.

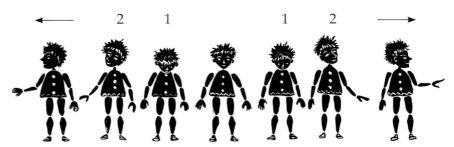

2   1   1   2

Wie bei der menschlichen Kopfbewegung vollzieht sich die Drehung in der Reihenfolge:
- senken
- kippen
- drehen
- aufrichten

Just like a human movement of the head, the turn takes place in the following order:
- lowering
- tilting
- turning
- straightening up

Die Kopfdrehung

Symbolisch stellt der Spielkreuzgriff den Kopf und der Ring zwischen Griff und Schulterschwinge den Hals der Marionette dar.

① Beugen Sie den Griff leicht nach vorn - und der Kopf unten senkt sich.

② Wenn Sie ihn nun nach rechts kippen, dreht sich der Kopf nach rechts und umgekehrt. Üben Sie die Drehung mit beiden Händen! Es bietet sich an, in der Drehung die Hand zu wechseln. Lassen Sie erneut die Marionette über den Teppich schweben und sie dabei mit entsprechenden Kopfbewegungen den Bühnenraum entdecken. Am jeweiligen Bühnenende wechseln Sie die Führungshand. Beginnen Sie diesen Wechsel mit einer Kopfdrehung, damit die Figur für den Zuschauer sichtbar den Entschluss zu einer Richtungsänderung fasst. Jede Handlung wird vom Kopf bestimmt und somit durch eine Kopfbewegung eingeleitet. Für den Richtungswechsel am Bühnenende wird die Kopfdrehung nun mit einer Körperdrehung kombiniert: Dabei drehen sich sowohl die Marionette als auch das Spielkreuz um eine Achse, die senkrecht durch Körper, Hals, Kopf und oben durch den Ring (= Hals) führt. In der Drehung wechseln Sie die Hand und lassen dann die Marionette zurückschweben.

The movement of the head

Symbolically the control bar handle represents the head and the ring between handle and shoulder pendulum represents the neck of the marionette.

① Lower the handle slightly to the front in order to lower the head of the puppet.

② If you now turn it to the right the head will turn to the right and vice versa. Practise the turn with both hands! It is advisable to change hands while turning. Let the marionette float over the carpet again and allow it to discover the stage area with appropriate movements of the head. Change hands each time you reach the end of the stage. Start this change with a turn of the head so that the figure – visible for the onlooker – makes the decision to turn right. Each human action is determined by the mind and thus initiated by a movement of the head. In order to carry out the change of direction at the end of the stage the turn of the head is now combined with a turn of the body. For this, the marionette as well as the control bar turn about an axis which leads vertically through body, neck, head and through the ring (= neck) at the top. Change to the other hand while turning and let the marionette float back.

Alle vier Finger einer Hand halten den Spielkreuzgriff ...

The control bar handle is helt by all four fingers ot a hand ..

Das Laufen

Beim Gehen und Laufen bewegt sich das menschliche Becken in einer sanften Wellen-linie. Sie entsteht durch das Strecken und Beu-gen der Beine bei gleichzeitigem Vorschieben des Beckens. Indem Sie das Spielkreuz in dieser Wellenlinie bewegen, schaffen Sie die Voraus-setzung für ein schönes Laufen.

① Drehen Sie mit dem Daumen die Bein-schwinge nach rechts und heben somit das linke Bein der Figur an.

② Nun schieben Sie das Spielkreuz um die gewünschte Schrittlänge nach vorn *und* nach unten – bis der Mari-onettenfuß aufsetzt.

③ Lassen Sie nun die Beinschwinge für einen Augenblick los und schieben das Spielkreuz wieder nach vorn *und* nach oben. Dadurch streckt sich das rech-te Bein.

④ In dem Moment, in dem es sich vom Boden löst, drehen Sie die Beinschwin-ge nach links und wiederholen nun den Vorgang mit dem rechten Bein, usw. Lassen Sie anfangs die Marionette lang-sam in großen Schrit-ten laufen und ach-ten Sie dabei auf die Wellenlinie des Lau-fens. Später können Sie die Schrittgröße der Figur anpassen.

Walking

When going or walking, the human pelvis moves in a gentle wavy line. This line is caused by stretching and bending the legs and simul-taneous pushing the pelvis forward. By moving the control bar along this line you create the preconditions for natural walking.

① Turn the leg pendulum to the right with your thumb and thus raise the left leg.

② Now push the control bar to the front by the desired step length *and* downwards – until the puppet's foot is put on the floor.

③ Then release the leg pendulum for a short moment and push the control bar to the front *and* up again. By doing so the right leg is straightened.

④ At the very mo-ment when the foot is raised from the floor turn the leg pendulum to the left and repeat this exercise with the right leg, etc. In the beginning, let the marionette walk slowly in the biggest strides possible and take care of the wavy line of walking.

... und der Dau-men bewegt die Beinschwinge.

... and the thumb moves the leg pendu-lum.

1   2   3

Die Verbeugung

Der Rückenfaden führt zum Becken der Marionette und somit zu ihrem Schwerpunkt, dem Ausgangspunkt sämtlicher Bewegungen. Oben im Spielkreuz symbolisiert der Rückenfaden das Rückgrat.

① Gleiten Sie mit Zeige- und Mittelfinger Ihrer freien Hand den Rückenfaden hinunter, bis Sie etwa am imaginären Becken sind (diese Distanz entspricht ungefähr der Rückenlänge der Marionette). Spannen Sie den Faden leicht an und die Marionette unten beginnt sich zu verbeugen!

② Eine Verbeugung ist im Prinzip eine Viertelkreisbewegung von Schulter und Kopf (= Spielkreuz) um das Becken als Mittelpunkt (= Finger Ihrer zweiten Hand).

③ Um zu verhindern, dass in der Verbeugung Ihre Finger wieder den Rückenfaden hinaufgleiten, bauen Sie ein Kräftegleichgewicht auf: die Hand, die das Spielkreuz hält, drückt nach vorn, und die Rückenfadenhand zieht mit gleicher Kraft dagegen. Stellen Sie sich vor, dass Sie einen Bogen spannen.

The bow

The back string leads to the marionette's pelvis and therefore to its centre of gravity, the starting point of all movements. At the control bar, the back string symbolizes the spine.

① Slide the fore and middle finger of your free hand down the back string until they nearly reach the imaginary pelvis (this distance approximately corresponds to the length of the marionette's back).

② Tighten the string slightly and the marionette begins to bow! In theory, a bow is a quarter circle movement of shoulder and head (= control bar) around the pelvis as axis (= fingers of your second hand).

③ In order to prevent your fingers from sliding back up the back string while the puppet bows, establish a balance of power by pushing your control bar hand to the front and letting the back string hand pull against it with the same energy.

Dem Rückenfaden kommt im Spiel eine groß Bedeutung zu. Da er zum Schwerpunkt der Figur führt sind mit ihm ausdrucksstarke Stellungen möglich.

The back string is of great significance. As it leads to the marionette's centre of gravity it enables expressive positions.

Die Armausleger

Mit den Armauslegern regelt man die Grundeinstellung der Hände. Sie lassen sich stufenlos in alle Richtungen einstellen. Weil sie am Kopfholz befestigt sind, lassen sich Hand- und Kopfbewegung auf vielfältige Weise miteinander verknüpfen. Stellen Sie die Ausleger wie auf dem Foto abgebildet ein. Machen Sie eine Verbeugung wie oben beschrieben. Wenn Sie jetzt den Kopf nach rechts drehen, hebt sich auch die rechte Hand. Drehen Sie den Kopf nach links, senkt sich die rechte Hand und die linke hebt sich.

Lassen Sie die Marionette den Boden um sich herum absuchen. Schulter und Kopf beschreiben dabei einen horizontalen Halbkreis um das Becken. Jede Richtungsänderung wird wieder durch die Kopfdrehung eingeleitet. Entdecken Sie, welche Bewegungsvielfalt nur durch ein simples Drehen und Wenden des Kreuzes möglich wird. Knien Sie nun mit der Marionette nieder, indem Sie die Rückenfadenhand und die Spielkreuzhand parallel nach vorn und unten schieben. Wenn Sie jetzt, wie abgebildet, das Spielkreuz nach vorn ziehen und gleichzeitig hin und her drehen und dabei die Hände der Figur auf dem Boden absetzen, krabbelt die Marionette.

The arm jibs

The basic adjustment of the hands is controlled by the arm jibs. They are fully adjustable in all directions. As they are fixed to the head bar, the movements of hand and head can be combined with each other in a varied manner. Adjust the jibs as demonstrated in the picture. Carry out a bow as described above. If you now turn the head to the right, the right hand is raised, too. If you turn it to the left the right hand is lowered and the left hand raised. Let the marionette examine the floor around itself. Shoulder and head will describe a horizontal semicircle around the pelvis. Each change of direction is again commenced by a turning of the head. Find out about the variety of movement that can be carried out by simply turning the control bar. Kneel down with your marionette now by parallel pushing the back string hand and the control bar hand to the front and down. You will make the marionette crawl if you now pull the control bar to the front – as demonstrated in the picture – and at the same time turn to and fro and put the hands of the marionette on the floor.

Sind, wie hier, die Armausleger entsprechend eingestellt, bewegen sich Kopf, Arme und Hände synchron zueinander – nur durch Drehung des Spielkreuzes bei gleichzeitigem Halten des Rückenfadens.

If the arm jibs are adjusted appropriately, as to be seen here, head, body, arms and hands can be moved simultaniously by just turning the control bar and holding the back string at the same time.

1   2   3   ⟶   4

Das Aufstehen

① Die Marionette kniet auf dem Boden. Ihre Hände befinden sich neben den Knien und damit dicht am Schwerpunkt.

② Fassen Sie nun den Rückenfaden an der entsprechenden Stelle, senken Sie das Spielkreuz, damit sich die Marionette mit den Händen abstützt.

Nun kommt es zu einer Gegenbewegung:

③ Die Spielkreuzhand bleibt genau in dieser Position, während die Rückenfadenhand wie ein Lift senkrecht nach oben geht.

④ Erst wenn die Beine der Marionette gestreckt sind-, dürfen sich ihre Hände vom Boden lösen. Wie bei der Verbeugung beschreiben dabei Schulter und Kopf ein Kreissegment um das Becken als Mittelpunkt.

Getting up

① The marionette kneels on the floor. Its hands are next to its knees and thus close to the centre of gravity.

② Now touch the back string at the appropriate spot, lower the control bar so that the puppet supports itself with its hands.

③ The countermovement is started: the control bar hand rests in exactly this position, while the back string hand moves vertically up like a lift.

④ Only if the marionette's legs are straightened, the hands can remove from the floor. As described for the bow, shoulders and head perform a circle segment around the pelvis as centre.

Zwischen Rückenfaden- und Spielkreuzhand wird ein Kräftegleichgewicht aufgebaut.

A balance of power is established between backstring hand and controllbar hand.

Die Handbewegung

Viele Handbewegungen ergeben sich aus dem Drehen und Wenden des Spielkreuzes nach vorheriger Einstellung der Armausleger. Für differenziertere Bewegungen gibt es noch ein Unterspielkreuz.

Im Handholz spiegelt sich die Marionettenhand: hinten das Handgelenk, vorn an der Innenseite des Querholzes der Zeigefinger, an der Außenseite der kleine Finger.

Es gibt zwei Arten der Handbewegung.

Vom Körper weg: Greifen Sie dazu mit Ihrer freien Hand von außen an das hintere Ende des Handholzes. Die rechte Hand führt die rechte Marionettenhand.

① Eine Auf- und Abbewegung der Hand erzeugt ein Winken, ein Drehen des Handholzes ein Drehen der Hand.

② Ein forsches Ziehen nach außen ergibt ein Zeigen. Aber achten Sie auf die Kopfhaltung! Nur wenn die Figur in die Richtung schaut, in die sie winkt oder zeigt, ist die Geste für den Zuschauer überzeugend.

Die zweite Art der Handbewegung ist zum Körper oder Kopf hin:

③ Hierzu greift Ihre freie Hand von oben durch die Ausleger hindurch das Handholz der gegenüberliegenden Hand und zieht sie beispielsweise zum Kopf hin. Auch in diesem Fall wirkt die Geste nur, wenn die Marionette auf ihre Spielhand schaut und mit dem Kopf der Hand leicht entgegenkommt.

The movement of the hand

Many movements of the hand result from turning the control bar after previous adjustment of the arm jibs. But for more differentiated movements a second control bar is available. Imagine the hand to be reproduced in the hand bar: the wrist at the back, the forefinger in front at the one side of the cross bar and the little finger at the other side.

There are two types of movements of the hand. Away from the body: In this case, you direct the marionette's right hand with your right hand while your left hand holds the control bar and vice versa.

① Moving the hand up and down creates a waving; turning the hand bar results in turning the marionette's hand and

② a firm outward pulling makes the marionette point. But again the turn of the head plays a decisive role. Only if the figure looks in the same direction as it waves or points to, the onlooker will have the impression that this gesture is convincing.

The second type of movement of the hand is towards body or head:

③ To let the puppet do so, your free hand grasps the hand at the imaginary forefinger through the arm jibs from above and for example pulls it towards the head. In this case, too, this gesture is only effective if the marionette looks at the hand and slightly moves towards it.

Jede Hand hat ein eigenes Unterspielkreuz, mit dem sie sehr differenziert bewegt werden kann.

Each hand has its own second control bar and can thus be moved in a very differentiated manner.

Die Augen, der Blick, das Ich, das Du, das Ihr. The eyes, the look, the me, the you.

Ohne Kleider wird das Wesentliche sichtbar.   Without clothes, the essence becomes visible.

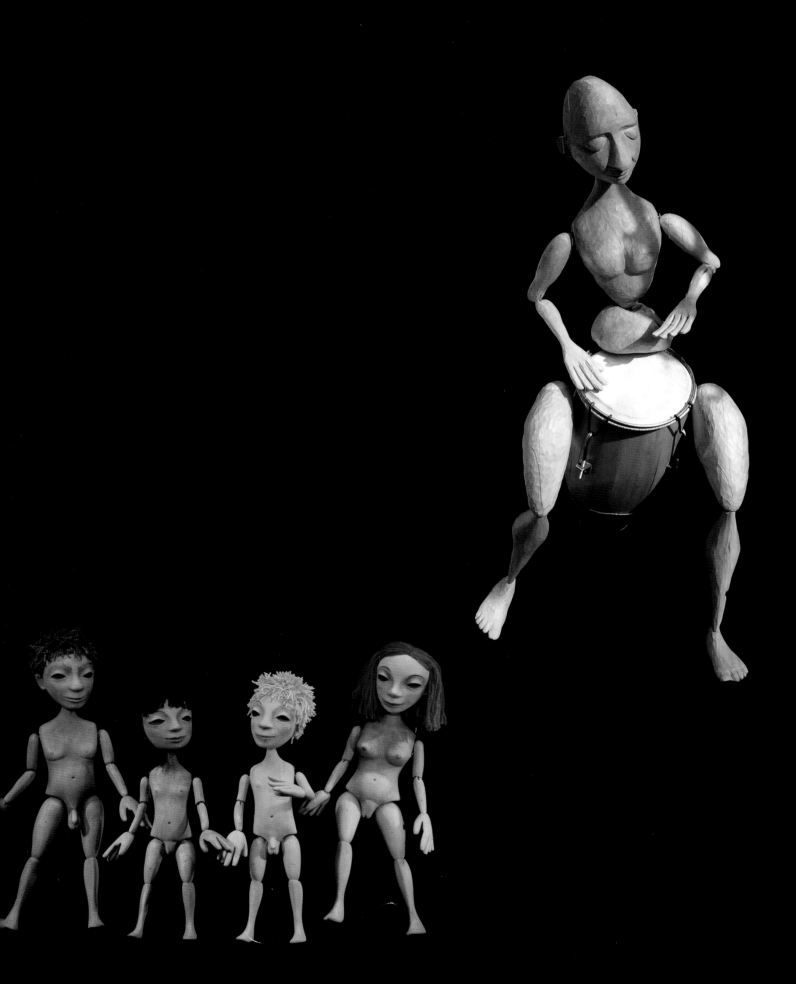

Schwerelos   Weightless

Die Marionette ist ein Wesen der Luft.

A marionette is a being of the air.

Don Quichotte oder das kleine Eselein –
wer ein Königreich erringen will, muss in die
Welt hinaus.

Whether Don Quixote or the Little Donkey –
anyone wanting to gain a kingdom must
venture forth into the world.

Die blaue Stunde   The blue hour

Der Monddrache berührt innere Welten.   The Moon Dragon touches on inner worlds.

Die Pendel-Spiel-kurse und das Pendel-Marionetten-Festival

The Pendel marionette courses and the Pendel marionette festival

Natürlich kann man Pendel-Marionetten als Kunstobjekte betrachten und sich daran erfreuen. Ihr eigentlicher Sinn aber ist das Spiel. Zu diesem Zweck wurden sie mit viel Sorgfalt gebaut. Auch für den Laien sind sie einfach zu handhaben. Ein in sich verstellbares Spielkreuz und eine ausgeklügelte Gelenktechnik ermöglichen verblüffend natürliche Bewegungsabläufe.

Marlene Gmelin und Detlef Schmelz wissen aus Erfahrung, wie vielschichtig die Marionette auf den Menschen wirken kann. Um dieses Wissen weiterzugeben, bieten sie seit Langem Seminare für Marionettenspiel an.

It is naturally possible to view Pendel-Marionettes as art objects and to take pleasure in them on that level. Their real purpose, though, is to be played. And to this end, they have been constructed with great care. Also for non-professionals, they are easy to handle. An adjustable control bar and a sophisticated joint structure allow the creation of astoundingly natural movements. Marlene Gmelin and Detlef Schmelz know from experience how complex the impact of marionettes on people can be. In order to pass on this knowledge, they have been offering courses in marionette playing for many years.

Mit Kugeln an einem Faden werden die Grundlagen de Marionetten- spiels eingeübt

The basics of marionette playing are practised with balls on a strin

Dort lernen die Teilnehmer zunächst an einfachen Einfaden-Marionetten, wie man eine Figur ruhig und sicher führt und wie man sich selbst dazu bewegt. Mit Tücherfiguren zu Musik erobert man anschließend den Raum und lernt in großen freien Bewegungen mit der Marionette zu tanzen.

Beginning with simple, single-string marionettes, the course participants learn first of all how to handle a figure smoothly and with assurance and how they themselves should move in the process. Subsequently, using cloth figures and accompanied by music, they conquer three-dimensional space, learning to dance with the marionette in broad, free movements.

Mit einer stilisierten Menschengestalt aus einem Seidentuch und fünf Kugeln erlernt man die koordinierte Bewegung mehrerer Pendel.

With a stylized human figure fashioned out of a silk cloth and five balls, students learn the coordinated movement of several pendulums.

Im nächsten Schritt wird die sogenannte Vollmarionette, die den Menschen abbildet, erklärt und es werden verschiedenste Bewegungen eingeübt. Dazu muss der Spielende sich in die Marionette hineinversetzen. Er macht sich scheinbar einfache Bewegungsabläufe wie das Gehen bewusst, um die Marionette in der Wellenlinie des Laufens bewegen zu können. Er bewegt sie erst langsam Schritt für Schritt, dann immer fließender und intuitiver.

As the next step, the players move on to full marionettes depicting the human figure. These are first explained, and each individual movement is then practised. The player must thereby put himself in the position of the marionette and become consciously aware of seemingly simple movement sequences. In the case of walking, for example, he must learn to move the marionette in the wavy line that naturally occurs, at first proceeding slowly, step by step, and then gradually increasing in speed until the motion becomes smooth and intuitive.

Die Vollmarionette und die Funktion des Spielkreuzes werden erklärt.

The full marionette and the function of the control bar are explained.

Den Ablauf dieser Bewegungen kann man an seinem eigenen Körper nachvollziehen. Sämtliche Fragen, die im Spiel auftreten, lassen sich so beantworten. Vereinfacht gesagt, um mit der Marionette zu spielen, ergründet man das eigene Laufen, das Sehen und die Gestik. Diese grundlegenden Fragen haben sich die Teilnehmer in der Regel so noch nie gestellt.

Die Marionette ist ein Wesen der Luft. Um mit ihr überzeugend zu laufen und zu handeln, muss die Schwerkraft vorgetäuscht werden. Dann wirkt sie eigenständig und lebendig. Mit der Übung wird das immer selbstverständlicher, und es entsteht nach und nach eine vitale Beziehung zwischen der Figur und dem Spieler. Von diesem gehen die Impulse aus, er führt die Marionette, aber letztlich dient er ihr; seine Aufgabe ist es, sie so zu beseelen, dass er die Welt aus ihren Augen heraus erblickt und für sie handelt.

So erfährt man im Üben mit der Marionette Wesentliches über die eigenen Bewegungsabläufe, über Pantomime und Theater.

It is possible to observe these movement sequences from one's own body. Indeed, all the questions that arise during playing can be answered in this way. Put another way: Playing a marionette means exploring one's own way of walking and seeing and one's own gestures. These are fundamental questions, but ones which most people have never asked themselves in this way.

Marionettes are creatures of the air. To enable them to walk and act convincingly, it is necessary to simulate gravity. They then appear to take on a life of their own.

With increasing practice, this becomes more and more natural, and a living relationship gradually develops between the figure and the player. And while it is the player who gives the impulses and guides the marionette, he is ultimately its servant; it is his task to breathe life into it, such that he sees the world through its eyes and acts on its behalf.

So in practising handling a marionette, one also acquires fundamental knowledge about one's own movements, about pantomime and about theatre.

Im Marionettenspiel geht es nicht nur um die Führung der Marionette, sondern auch um die eigene Körperhaltung.

Marionette playing is not only about handling the marionette; it is also about one's own body posture.

Für viele ist es überraschend und spannend, wie das Marionettenspiel von den eigenen Bewegungen bestimmt wird und wie man umgekehrt im Spiel mit der Marionette sich des eigenen Körpers, der eigenen Bewegungen bewusst wird. Die Marionette spiegelt den Spieler und umgekehrt findet sich der Spielende in der Marionette wieder. Sind beide in Einklang, entsteht ein harmonisches Spiel, das den Charakter der Figur aufnimmt. Eine grazile Tänzerin hat nicht nur einen ganz anderen Bewegungsduktus als ein derber Räuber, sondern sie unterscheidet sich von ihm auch in ihrem Denken, Fühlen und Handeln wesentlich. Sie ist eine gänzlich andere Person, in die sich der Spieler einzufinden hat.

For many people, it is surprising and fascinating to see how marionette playing is determined by one's own movements and how, conversely, marionette playing makes one aware of one's own body

and one's own movements. The marionette is a reflection of the player, and at the same time, the player finds himself in the marionette. Where the two are in accord, the result is harmonious playing that picks up the character of the figure. A graceful dancer has not only a completely different movement pattern from a rough and tough robber, she also differs from him in her thinking, feeling and doing. She is a completely different person, with whom the player must identify.

In den Spielkursen erlernen die Teilnehmer das Marionettenspiel. Zu Hause erleben sie – meist zunächst im kleinen Kreis –, wie fasziniert die Zuschauer auf ihr Spiel reagieren. So schöpfen sie immer mehr Mut, entwickeln eigene Spielideen und spielen zu Festen und anderen Gelegenheiten.

In the courses, the participants learn the techniques of marionette playing. But at home – usually, at first, within only a small circle of people – they experience how fascinated the spectators are by their performance. As a consequence, they gain ever more courage, develop their own ideas, and play at festive gatherings and on other occasions.

Das Spiel auf engem Raum erfordert eine gegenseitige Absprache und Achtung.

Playing in confined spaces calls for mutual accord and respect.

In den Fortgeschrittenenkursen werden diese Ansätze weiterentwickelt. Die Teilnehmer sehen die eigenen Fortschritte und die der anderen und lernen voneinander. Fast spielerisch findet jeder seine persönliche Art und Weise, mit der Marionette umzugehen. Das ist konzentrierte Arbeit und bleibt dennoch eine spannende und gleichzeitig entspannende Beschäftigung.
Später, in den Theaterkursen, wird es professioneller. Die Szenen werden weiter verfeinert und die Spieler beschäftigen sich eingehend mit der Wirkung von Licht und Schatten, den Mitteln der Bühnentechnik, dem Ton und der Sprache.

In the advanced courses, these basic skills are developed further. The students see their own progress and that of the others, and learn from each other. Almost without effort, everyone finds their own personal way of handling the marionette. This is task that calls for great concentration, but one that provides excitement and relaxation at the same time.
Later, in the theatre courses, things become more professional still; the scenes become more elaborate, and the players look in detail at the effects of light and shade, the use of stage equipment and the resources of sound and language.

Erst im Theaterlicht kommt die Marionette voll zur Geltung.

The marionette is fully effective only in the theatre light.

Die Spieler beseelen die Marionetten, denken, fühlen und handeln für sie.

The players breathe life into the marionettes – thinking, feeling and acting in their stead.

Für viele wird die Marionette zu einem wertvollen Ausdrucksmittel. Im Spiel erleben die Teilnehmer die subtile Wirkung der Marionette auf die Menschen. Ihr gegenüber öffnen sich Kinder und Erwachsene und lassen bereitwillig Nähe und Berührungen zu. Mit ihr kann man Dinge sagen, die im direkten Gespräch nicht möglich wären, und mit ihr lassen sich behutsam Verhaltensweisen aufzeigen, ohne das Gegenüber zu verletzen. So kommt es, dass nicht wenige Spielkurs-Teilnehmer die Marionette in ihren Beruf integrieren. Sie findet Verwendung in Pädagogik, Medizin, Psychologie, Altenpflege und vielen anderen Bereichen.

For many people, as a result, the marionette becomes a valuable means of expression. In the course of performing, the participants experience for themselves the subtle effects that marionettes can have on people. Children and adults are much more likely to open up to them and readily accept closeness and contact. With a marionette, it is possible to say things that could never be said in direct conversation, and also to unobtrusively demonstrate types of behaviour without causing offence to the other person. It is therefore not surprising that marionettes are used by many professionals in their work, and not only in education and psychology, but also medicine, geriatrics and many other fields.

A marionette player ...
must have a sure feeling for gestures.
Gestures must be clear, but must be used sparingly so as not to become worn out.

Marcel Marceau

Im Umgang mit der Marionette macht jeder eigene Erfahrungen und entwickelt aufgrund seiner individuellen Fähigkeiten einen eigenen Stil. Auf diese Weise entstanden aus den Kursen heraus in ganz Deutschland und den Nachbarländern zahlreiche Spielinitiativen und wunderbar vielfältige Marionettentheater. Manche bleiben eher im kleineren Rahmen, andere entwickeln sich zu selbstständigen Theatern. Sie eint die Freude am Marionettenspiel und oft agieren sie auf hohem Niveau. Und alle erwecken Pendel-Marionetten zum Leben.

In working with a marionette, everyone acquires their own experience and develops their own style on the strength of their own abilities. As a result, the courses have given rise to a considerable number of wonderfully varied marionette theatre activities and playing initiatives in the whole of Germany and the neighbouring countries. Some former participants have continued their activities on a relatively small in scale, while others have built up their own theatres. What they all have in common, however, is pleasure in marionette playing, and very often to a high standard. But in all cases, they play with Pendel figures and succeed in bringing them to life.

Der Marionettenspieler ...
muss ein sicheres Gespür für die Gestik haben.
Die Geste muss eindeutig sein,
sparsam verwendet werden,
damit sie sich nicht verbraucht.

Marcel Marceau

Es klopft bei Wanja in der Nacht: In den Spielkursen werden Schulstücke angeboten, in denen man das Spiel in der Gruppe erlernt.

In the night, there is a knock on Vanya's door: The marionetteering courses also include school plays, allowing the participants to learn to play as part of a group.

Um den Spielkursteilnehmern Bühnenerfahrung zu ermöglichen, entstand die Idee, gemeinsam ein Marionettenfestival zu veranstalten.

Schon das erste Pendel-Marionetten-Festival 2008 wurde ein großer Erfolg. Seitdem findet es alle 2 Jahre statt. Drei Tage lang wird für Jung und Alt eine wunderbare Vielfalt an Inszenierungen geboten.

At some time in the course of 2008, the idea simply arose of organizing a festival with all these theatres and initiatives – and the Pendel-Marionette-Festival was born. The very first event was already a great success. It lasted for three days and was a wonderful collaboration between young and old. And it has stayed that way ever since, being held every two years in the autumn of each even-numbered year.

Das Festival – eine zauberhafte Welt der Fantasie.

The Festival – a magical world of the imagination.

Zur Aufführung kommen Kindergeschichten, Fabeln, Märchen und Mythen bis hin zu literarischen Werken und der satirischen Aufbereitung zeitgenössischer Themen. Es entfaltet sich eine Welt der Fantasie und Poesie.

So individuell wie die Darbietenden sind die Spielformen. Einige spielen allein oder zu mehreren komplexe Inszenierungen, andere führen eine kleine Szene im Rahmen eines Szenenprogramms auf oder nehmen an den Gemeinschaftsstücken teil. Das ganze Haus ist erfüllt von Spielfreude.

Höhepunkt eines jeden Festivals bildet das große Gemeinschaftsstück. Geplant und vorbereitet von einigen wenigen, wird es mit vielen Teilnehmern über einen langen Zeitraum von ein bis zwei Jahren in den Spielkursen eingeübt und gestaltet.

It is aimed at all age groups and offers a fantastic variety of marionette performance: from picture book stories, fables, fairy tales, myths and fantasy stories full of poetry, to literary and satirical subjects.

The modes of performance are equally varied: Some players play solo or form groups and put on more complex productions, while others present one scene as part of a bigger programme, or take part in one of the many joint productions. Every participant finds an opportunity to appear at least once or probably several times. Wherever one looks, the marionettes are brought to life, creating a magical world of the imagination. The high point of each festival is the great joint production. Though planned and prepared by just a few, it is practised and perfected with a large number of participants and over a long period of time – one or two years – in the marionette courses.

Das Pendel-Marionetten-Festival findet alle zwei Jahre statt, immer im Herbst der Jahre mit gerader Jahreszahl. Festivalort ist das Seminarhaus von Hohebuch/Waldenburg bei Schwäbisch Hall. Weitere Informationen zum Festival und den Spielkursen: www.pendel-marionetten.de

The Pendel-Marionette-Festival is held every two years, always in autumn and always in years with an even number. The venue is the course centre in Hohebuch/Waldenburg near Schwäbisch Hall. For further information on the festival and the courses, please go to www.pendel-marionetten.de

Aus dem Hauptprogramm des Pendel-Marionetten-Festivals 2012

Some highlights from the main programme of the 2012 Pendel-Marionette-Festival

…ärentheater,
…r. Bernhard Betz,
…schwang

…ärenikes
…lavierstunde

…ärenikes
…iano lesson

Marionetten-
theater
Löwenzahn,
Elisabeth Schnorr
und Ute Jakobi,
Bad Vilbel

Ein erhebender
Tag im Leben
des Frosches
Fri-do-ling

An uplifting day
in the life of
Fri-do-ling Frog

…ageworks
…uppets,
…aniela Schulz
…nd Harry De Lon,
…ünchen

…as Geheimnis
…er Fuchsmaske

…he mystery of the
…x mask

Marionetten-
theater
Zauberfaden,
Christel Albrecht,
Lautenbach

Aufregung
am Froschteich

Commotion at
frog pond

…arionettenspiel
…agibi,
…atherine Cunz,
…ürich

…er Junge,
…as Mädchen und
…er Hund

…he boy, the girl
…nd the dog

Marionetten-
theater Eule
und Meerkatze
Dr. Angelika
Steveling und
Dr. Ulrich
Kordes, Essen

Till
Eulenspiegel

Till
Eulenspiegel

Klimakonferenz in New York. Wochenlang hat
es geregnet. Der Freiheitsstatue steht das Wasser bis zum Hals. Italienische Gondolieri regeln
den Schiffsverkehr auf der 5th Avenue. Der
Konferenzort, das UNO-Hauptquartier, ist
dicht umlagert von Demonstranten und Um-
weltaktivisten auf Flößen, Booten und allem,
was schwimmt. Auf einem großen Ponton
gibt Bob Dylan ein Konzert, so wie damals in
Woodstock.
Zur Liveberichterstattung hat der Sender
Planet Earth Media die ehrgeizige Reporterin
Janine Pfotenschnell geschickt. Sie wird begleitet von dem etwas tollpatschigen Kameramann
Eddie Behrmann. Auf dem Weg zur Konferenz
hoch oben im UNO-Gebäude interviewt sie
alle, die Rang und Namen haben: Politiker,
Vertreter der Wirtschaft und Lobbyisten. Diese
Experten haben nur ihre eigenen Interessen im
Blick. Hinter ihren Floskeln versteckt sich eine
hanebüchene Weltsicht.
Zum Beispiel hat Professor Ohnesorg von der
Atomindustrie einen äußerst kreativen Vor-
schlag für die Wiederverwertung abgelaufe-
ner Brennstäbe. Dr. Gockel sieht die positiven
Seiten der dramatischen Polabschmelzungen,
weil man endlich an die riesigen Öl- und Gas-
vorkommen unter dem Eis kommt. Und der
Wirtschaftslobbyist Wolfgang Grimm hält es
für endgültig widerlegt, dass Kohlendioxid für
die Klimaerwärmung verantwortlich sei.

Climate change conference in New York. It's
been raining for weeks. The Statue of Liberty
is up to its neck in water. Italian gondoliers are
now responsible for controlling the boat traf-
fic on 5th Avenue. The conference venue, the
UN headquarters building, is surrounded by
crowds of demonstrators and environmental
activists on and in rafts, boats and anything
else that will float. On a giant pontoon, Bob
Dylan is giving a concert - reminiscences of
Woodstock.
To report live from the scene, the TV station
Planet Earth Media has sent their ambitious
reporter Janine Lightpaw. She is accompanied
by her somewhat ungainly cameraman Eddie
Bearman. On the way to the conference, to be
held high up in the UN building, she interviews everybody who is anybody: politicians,
representatives of the business community,
lobbyists. These experts only have an eye for
their own interests. Their statements reveal a
hair-raising attitude towards the world and the
current situation.
Professor Clueless of the nuclear industry, for
example, has a highly creative proposal on the
uses to which spent fuel rods can be put.
Dr. Cockerel sees the positive sides to the dra-
matic melting of the polar ice caps, as it means
that it will finally be possible to access the huge
oil and gas reserves located beneath the ice.
And business lobbyist Wolf Grim asserts that
the argument that carbon dioxide is responsible
for global warming has been finally laid to rest.
Planet Earth Media is a commercial broadcas-
ter. The interviews are interrupted by adver-
tising and are illustrated with background
reports. On-the-spot reporters talk to children
combing through rubbish on the flooded coasts
of the Himalayas, observe thirsty frogs buying
water from a fat toad at inflated prices, and
show penguins who have been provided with
refrigerators as an emergency measure to enable them to make ice cubes.
As a journalist, Ms. Lightpaw feels committed
to reporting objectively, but is increasingly beginning to question the sincerity of her intervie-
wees. On her way up though the building, she
repeatedly encounters two caretakers who are
looking for a screw that has come loose some-

Touristik
Herr Philipp
Sonnentag:
Kreuzfahrt im
Himalaya.

Tourism
Mr. Philipp
Sunnidays:
Cruises in the
Himalayas.

Forschung
Herr Dr. Mischa
Unbedarft:
Wissenschaft ist
klimaneutral.

Research
Dr.
Mike Dimwit:
Science is clima-
te neutral.

Finanz
Herr Direktor
Gernot Grau:
Wasserrechte
aufkaufen!

**Finance
Director**
Gerald Grey:
Buy water
rights!

Atom
Herr Prof.
Hans Ohnesorg:
Atomkraft ist
todsicher!

Nuclear
Prof.
Josh Clueless:
Nuclear energy
is a dead cert!

Experte
Herr Wolfgang
Grimm: Nur
keine Panik!
Es regelt sich
schon von
allein!

Expert
Mr. Wolf Grim:
Don't panic!
It will all sort
itself out!

Chemie
Frau Dr.
Gerlinde Fox:
Gensoja statt
Regenwald.

Chemistry
Dr. Getrie Fox:
Genetically
modified soya
in place of rain
forests.

Kurz vor der
offiziellen Eröff-
nung der Klima-
konferenz.

Shortly before
the opening of
the climate con-
ference.

Planet Earth Media ist ein werbefinanzierter
Sender. Die Interviews werden von Werbeclips
unterbrochen und mit Hintergrundberichten
illustriert. Vorort-Reporter sprechen mit Kin-
dern, die an den überschwemmten Küsten des
Himalaya Müll sammeln, beobachten dürsten-
de Frösche, die einer fetten Kröte teuer
Wasser abkaufen müssen, und zeigen Pinguine, denen als Sofortmaßnahme Kühlschränke
zur Herstellung von Eiswürfeln zur Verfügung
gestellt wurden.
Als Reporterin fühlt sich Janine Pfotenschnell
der objektiven Berichterstattung verpflichtet,
gerät aber immer mehr ins Zweifeln an der

Vollkommenes Marionettentheater ist
vollkommen körperlich gewordene Poesie ...
Da ist es möglich, dass eine Geige sich biegt
und anfängt zu tanzen,
dass ein Diener mit sechs Händen bedient,
dass ein Verliebter beim Anblick des Mädchens
den Kopf verliert ...

Motten stricken
Ölschutzpullo-
ver für Pinguine
in Not.

Moths knitting
oil protection
pullovers for
penguins in
need.

Omnia, das
Auto der Zu-
kunft zu Was-
ser, zu Land
und in der
Luft.

Omnia, the car
of the future, for
use on water,
on land and in
the air.

Sonnenbaden
auf den Spuren
des Dalai Lama.

Sunbathing in
the footsteps of
the Dalai Lama.

Abruptes Ende
der Klimakon-
ferenz.

Abrupt end
to the climate
conference.

Hut ab vor allen Mitspielern und guten Geistern hinter und zwischen den Kulissen!

Hats off to the players and all the other helpers behind and between the scenes!

Diese Inszenierung entstand über drei Jahre in den Spielkursen und wurde als großes Gemeinschaftsstück erstmals beim Festival 2012 aufgeführt. Aus diesem Stoff entsteht in Zusammenarbeit mit der Filmemacherin Lilo Mangelsdorff ein Kinofilm.

This performance was created in the marionette courses over a period of three years and was first presented as a joint, major work at the 2012 Festival. A cinema film based on the material is in the process of production in collaboration with film-maker Lilo Mangelsdorff.

Perfect marionette theatre is the perfect
incarnation of poetry:
All reality appears transformed,
the humans dehumanized, objects coming to life.
It becomes possible for a violin to bend
and begin to dance, for the waiting-on
to be done by a servant with six hands,
for a lover to lose his head
at the sight of his girl ...

Tankred Dorst

Pendel-
Marionetten-Theater

östlich der Sonne

Pendel
marionette theatre

east of the Sun
and west of the Moon

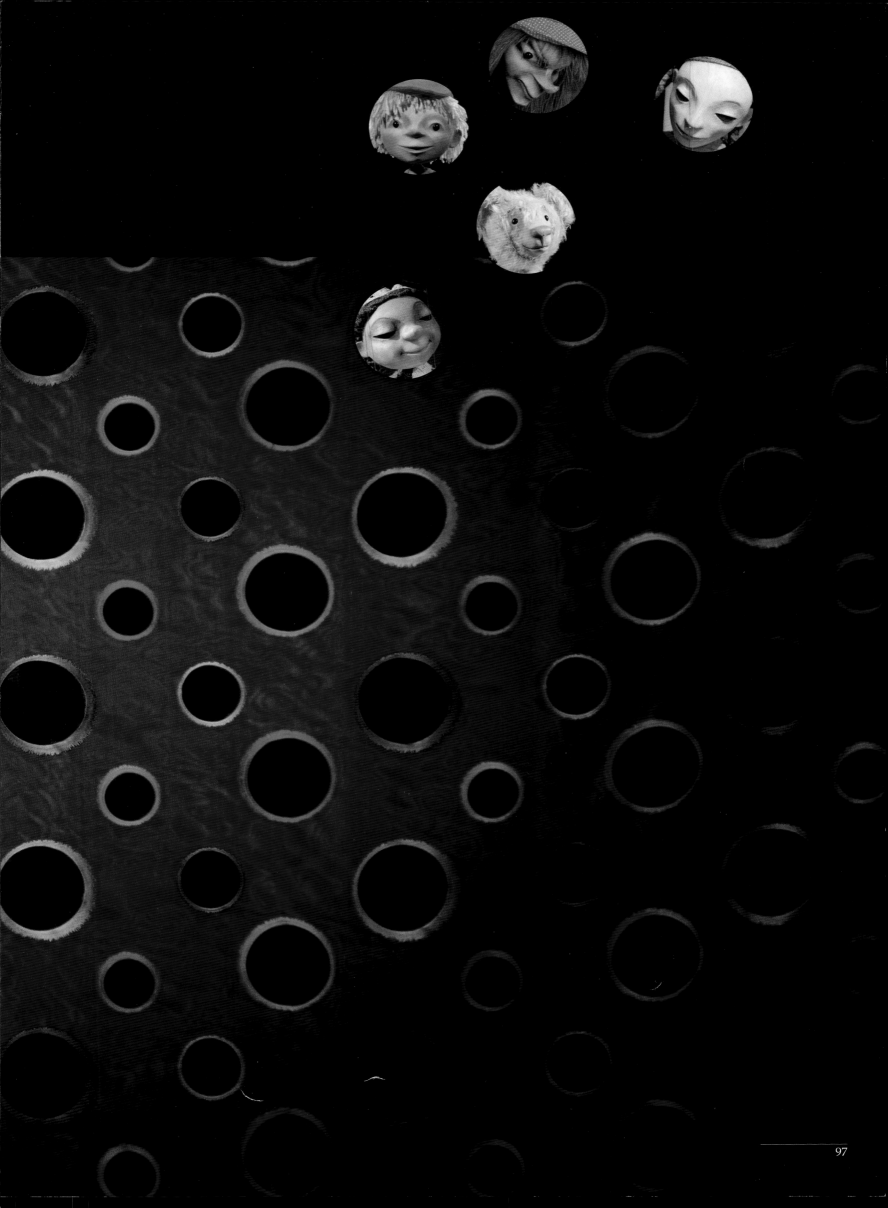

Geschichten ohne Worte

Stories without words

Das Spiel mit der Marionette,
erklärt am Beispiel unseres Szenenprogrammes
„Geschichten ohne Worte"

Als faszinierter Zuschauer eines guten Marionettenspiels glaubt man leicht, dass der Spieler
über große Fingerfertigkeiten verfügen muss.
Hat man jedoch einmal die Möglichkeit, die
Hände des Marionettenspielers zu beobachten,
wird man feststellen, dass sie relativ sparsame,
aber sehr gezielte Bewegungen ausführen.
Seine eigentliche Leistung hat der Marionettenspieler lange vor diesem Spiel vollbracht.
Er hat sich nämlich gefragt: Wie bewege ich
mich eigentlich? Was geht in meinem Körper
vor, wenn ich mich hinsetze, wenn ich aufstehe,
gehe, laufe, winke, schleiche, schaue, entdecke?
Sich selbst beobachtend, ist er sich über viele
seiner Bewegungsabläufe bewusst geworden
und hat dabei viel über sich, seine Gelenke
und seine Anatomie gelernt. So hat er sich mit
der Zeit ein Wissen über die eigene Bewegung
erarbeitet. Je mehr er jedoch darauf achte-
te, desto mehr fiel ihm auf, wie verschieden
sich die Menschen bewegen und welch feine
Unterschiede es gibt: Eine dicke Person läuft
ganz anders als eine dünne, eine cholerische
unterscheidet sich von einer sanguinischen,
eine träumerische bewegt sich ganz anders als
eine abenteuerlustige, ein Kind hüpft flink wie
ein Ball, ein Erwachsener geht eher bedächtig.
So ist dem Spieler bewusst geworden, dass er
nicht unbedingt seine eigenen Bewegungsmus-
ter auf die Marionette übertragen sollte, sondern sich in sie, in ihren Typus und Charakter
einfühlen muss. Deshalb beschäftigt er sich mit
der Persönlichkeit der zu spielenden Marionette und beginnt mit Zuschreibungen:
Otto ist vulgär und noch in der Pubertät. Er ist
ziemlich aufmüpfig und bewegt sich erdver-
bunden, jedoch trotz der Körperfülle schnell
und wendig. Er ist meist unausgeschlafen und
schlecht gelaunt, kann aber, wenn er will und
es zu seinem eigenen Nutzen sein könnte, sehr
charmant sein. Er bringt kaum einen richtigen
Satz zustande und kann Friede und Harmonie
nicht ausstehen. Er sucht den Streit.

The play with the marionette,
explained by example of our scene program
„Stories without Words"

As a fascinated onlooker of a good puppet-
show it is easy to believe that the master has
to possess very nimble fingers. But if you ever
have the opportunity to observe the hands of a
marionette master, you will observe that they
can make relatively few, but very selective,
movements. The puppet master has completed
all his real work long before the show. Name-
ly he has asked himself, „How do I actually
move? What happens within my body when I
sit down, stand up, walk, run, nod, crawl, look,
discover?" Looking at himself, he has become
aware of many of his movement sequences and
in doing so learnt a great deal about himself
and his joints and his anatomy. In this way,
with time, he will have developed a knowledge
of his own movements. The more attention he
paid to this however, the more it occurred to
him how differently people move and which
fine differences there are. A fat person runs
quite differently from a thin one, a choleric
person is different from a sanguinary person, a
dreamy person moves quite differently from an
adventurous one. A child hops along as nimble
as a ball, adults tend to be more deliberate in
their walk.
In this way he became aware that he shouldn't
necessarily transpose his own style of movement on to the puppet, but to emphasise with
the type and character of the puppet. For this
reason he involves himself with the personality of the puppet to be played and begins with
assigning the puppet a character.

Otto is vulgar and still going through puber-
ty. He is fairly rebellious and drags his feet,
however in spite of his ample frame he moves
quickly and is supple. He has rarely had a good
night's rest and is bad-tempered, however, he
can, if so inclined, and it could be to his advantage, be very charming. He hardly ever utters
a proper sentence and cannot stand peace and
harmony. He is looking for confrontation.

Ganz anders sind dagegen die Zuschreibungen für den Pantomimen Pic: Er ist schön anzusehen, leicht, fließend, tänzerisch in den Bewegungen, träumerisch in seine eigene Welt versunken, die Außenwelt fast gar nicht wahrnehmend. Er liebt das Ästhetische und entdeckt bewundernd das Schöne in seiner Umgebung. Er kann stundenlang einem Schmetterling zuschauen, ist sehr leise, scheu und vorsichtig. Er will die Stille genießen.

Schaut man nun noch einmal – mit diesem Wissen – dem Marionettenspieler zu, so wird man feststellen, dass in gewisser Weise die Figur, die er gerade spielt, sich unbewusst in seinen Bewegungen widerspiegelt: stampfender Gang, schnelle abrupte Bewegungen mit dem Körper und Schalk im Gesicht – so sieht man ihn den Punk spielen.

Lässt er nun Pic, den Pantomimen, die Bühne betreten, werden seine Bewegungen ruhig und entspannt, seine Schritte leicht und behutsam. In seiner Körperhaltung ähnelt er der Figur, die er führt, und er durchlebt in sich, was die Figur vorgibt zu erleben. Innerlich ist er unten in der Figur, ist quasi sie. Er spielt sie dann gut, wenn der Zuschauer ihn nicht wahrnimmt.

On the other hand the characters assigned for the „Pic" pantomimist are very different. He is attractive to look at, light, flowing, dancer-like in his movements, dreamily engrossed in his own world, hardly noticing the outside world at all. He loves the aesthetic and discovers what is beautiful in his surroundings with admiration. He can look at a butterfly for hours, is very quiet, shy, and cautious. He wants to enjoy tranquillity.

If you now look at the puppet player once more with this knowledge, you will ascertain that in a certain way the figure which he is playing at the moment is unconsciously reflected in his movements. Stamping his feet as he walks, quick, abrupt bodily movements with the facial expression of a rogue – in this way you see him playing the punk.

If he now allows Pic, the pantomimist onto the stage, his movements will be relaxed and smooth, his steps light and careful. His posture resembles that of the figure which he is controlling and he lives through what the figure purports to experience. In his soul he is down there in the figure. He then plays it well if he is not observed by the onlooker.

Hans Huckebein

Jetzt aber naht sich das Malheur,
Denn dies Getränke ist Likör.
Es duftet süß. – Hans Huckebein
Taucht seinen Schnabel froh hinein.
Und lässt mit stillvergnügtem Sinnen
Den ersten Schluck hinunterrinnen.
Nicht übel! – Und er taucht schon wieder
Den Schnabel in die Tiefe nieder.
Er hebt das Glas und schlürft den Rest,
Weil er nicht gern was übrig lässt.
Ei, ei! Ihm wird so wunderlich,
So leicht und doch absunderlich.
Er krächzt mit freudigem Getön
Und muss auf einem Beine stehn.
Der Vogel, welcher sonsten fleucht,
Wird hier zu einem Tier, was kreucht.
Und Übermut kommt zum Beschluss,
Der alles ruinieren muss.

Nach Wilhelm Busch

Hans Huckebein

Disaster's on its way, for sure,
For this libation is liqueur.
Inquisitive Hans Huckebein
Inserts his beak – this does smell fine!
Contentedly, he takes a nip
And wets his whistle with a sip.
Not bad at all! – he thinks, and then
His beak submerges once again.
He lifts the glass and slurps the rest
Because the last drop tastes the best.
This feeling is amazing,
So light, yet oddly dazing!
Quite merrily, he caws and crows,
Assuming a most graceful pose.
The bird, a creature of the wing,
Becomes a creeping, crawling thing.
To be more rowdy than one should
Will ruin everything for good.

By Wilhelm Busch

Hüah, hott,
so lauf doch!

Giddy-up! Giddy-up!
Come and let's go

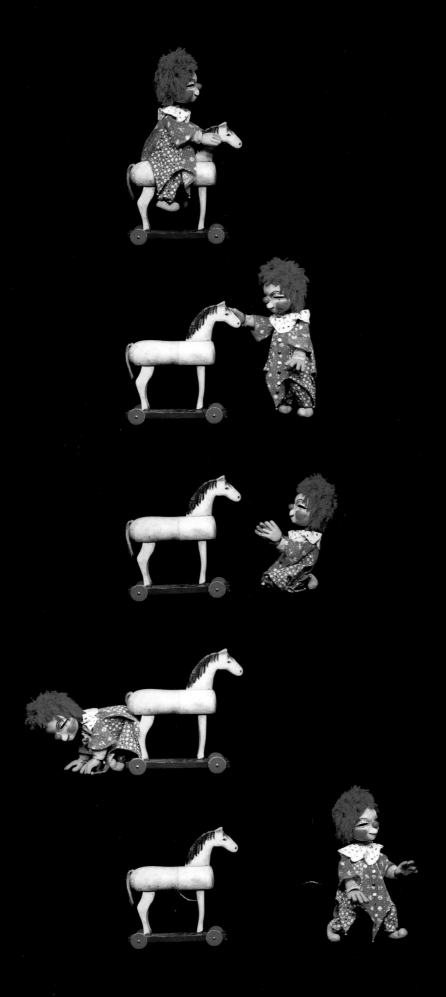

Ben, der Bär, und die Traumschiffsegler

Ben, the bear, and the dream fish sailors

Schwungvolle Zirkusmusik ertönt, der Zirkusdirektor begrüßt die erwartungsfrohen Zuschauer und – sagt die Vorstellung ab: „Es gibt keine Artisten!" Im letzten Augenblick aber erscheint Ben, der Bär, und bietet dem verblüfften Zirkusdirektor an, Tiere aus der ganzen Welt als Artisten zu holen. In seinem großen Fischschiff macht er sich sofort auf die Reise nach Afrika, findet dort einen Storch und einen Elefanten, in Asien zauberhafte Wesen aus dem Land der Morgenröte und in Australien ein Känguru und sogar einen Koalabären. In den großen Fliederwäldern Europas entdeckt er das sagenumwobene Einhorn, im Wilden Westen von Amerika einen waghalsigen Kojoten und in der Antarktis schließlich einen Pinguin, der gerade einen Kakadu ausbrütet. Von Land zu Land füllt sich das Fischschiff, bis es schließlich einer Arche Noah gleicht.

Bei seiner Rückkehr findet er im Zirkus nur noch einen einsamen, Geige spielenden Bären vor. Doch jetzt schlägt die Stimmung um. Die Vorstellung beginnt.

Lively circus music sounds; the circus director welcomes the expectunt audience and – cancels the performance: „We don't have any artists!" But in the very last moment Ben, the bear, appears and offers the astonished circus director to go and get animals from all over the world. At once he starts his journey in his big fish ship. In Africa he finds a stork, an elephant, in Asia enchanting creatures from the land of the red sky and in Australia a kangaroo und even a koala bear. In the big lilac woods of Europe he discovers the legendary unicorn, in the wild west of America a fearless coyote and finally in Antarctica a penguin, which is just hatching a cockatoo. From country to country the fish ship fills up until at last it looks like Noah's Arch. On his return, he only finds one bear in the circus, lonely playing the fiddle. But soon the mood is changing. The performance can take place.

ZIRKUS PENDOLINO

Das Publikum ist begeistert, denn die Tiere zeigen zauberhaft poetische Darbietungen. Der Elefant tanzt Walzer, der Pinguin dreht die Orgel, das Känguru jongliert, der Kojote turnt sensationell am Trapez und das Einhorn erscheint am Mondenteich ...

The audience is enthusiastic because the animals show enchanting poetic performances. The elephant dances the waltz, the penguin plays the barrel organ, the kangaroo juggles, the coyote does sensational exercises on the trapeze and the unicorn appears at the moon pond ...

... und mit einer spektakulären Einradnummer beschließt Ben, der Bär, die Vorstellung.

Fabeln am seidenen Faden
pantomimisch gespielt für Erwachsene und Kinder
Musik von Gregory Charamsa

... and with a spectacular unicycle act Ben, the bear, closes the performance.

An internationally comprohensible poetic puppet pantomime accompanied by music of Gregory Charamsa

Die Mäusebraut

The mouse bride

Ein Mäusepaar hatte eine wunderschöne Tochter, die nur mit dem Besten und Mächtigsten verheiratet werden sollte. Lange überlegten die Eltern, wer wohl infrage käme, aber sie fanden niemanden. Als jedoch einmal die Sonnenstrahlen in der Höhle tanzten, sprang Vater Maus auf und sprach: „Wir wollen den machtvollen Sonnenherrn fragen, ob er unsere Tochter zur Frau nehmen will. Er kann sie gewiss glücklich machen." Und er machte sich sogleich auf den Weg, um seinen Antrag dem Sonnenherrn zu unterbreiten.

A mice couple had a beautiful daughter who should be married only to the best and mightiest husband. They thought for a long while who would be worthy of consideration but couldn't find anybody. But when one day the sunbeams danced into the hole, father mouse jumped to his feet and said: „We will ask the mighty master of the sun whether he wants to take our daughter to wife. He surely will be able to make her happy." And he set off at once to present his proposal to the master of the sun.

„Sonnenherr, du Mächtiger! Du bist gewiss der großartigste Mann. Mama Maus und ich, wir haben beschlossen, unsere Tochter nur dem Allerstärksten zur Frau zu geben und so trage ich dir die Hand unserer Tochter an." Huldvoll schaute der Sonnenherr auf Papa Maus, sagte aber: „Ich muss zugeben, der Allerstärkste bin ich nicht immer. Es gibt jemanden, der meine Strahlen verdecken kann, sodass mich niemand auf der Erde sieht, und dann bin ich hilflos. – Es ist der Regen mit seiner dunklen Wolke." „Oh, wenn du nicht der Mächtigste bist, dann muss ich zum Regen laufen!", sagte Papa Maus und machte sich auf den Weg.
Als er endlich zum Regen kam, trug er ihm die Hand seiner Tochter an. Der Regen fühlte sich sehr geehrt, aber er senkte bescheiden den Kopf und sprach: „Es gibt jemanden, der noch mächtiger ist als ich. Wenn er bläst, zerteilt er meine Wolken und scheucht mich über die ganze Erde. Das ist der Wind!" „Dann muss ich den Wind fragen!", sagte Papa Maus und machte sich auf die Suche.
Nach weiten Wegen traf er den Wind und sagte zu ihm: „Wind, du bist gewiss der Mächtigste, du bist mächtiger als der Regen, mächtiger als der Sonnenherr, du bist der erwünschte Bräutigam für unsere Tochter!" Der Wind freute sich sehr über den Antrag. Doch er seufzte und sprach: „Ich wünschte, es wäre so, wie du sagst. Aber da ist jemand, wenn der mir im Weg steht, dann komme ich nicht weiter und muss ausweichen. Mächtiger als ich ist der Berg, auf dem du stehst."
Und Papa Maus purzelte vor Schreck den Berg hinunter.

„Mighty master of the sun! You certainly are the most brilliant of all men. Mother mouse and I, we decided that only the strongest man of all should be given our daughter to wife and so I offer you our daughter's hand." The master of the sun looked graciously at father mouse but said: „I have to admit that I am not always the strongest of all. There is someone who can cover my beams so that nobody on earth can see me and then I am helpless. – It's the rain with his dark cloud." „Oh, if you are not the mightiest man of all I have to go to the rain!", father mouse said and set off again.
When he came to the rain at last he offered him his daughter's hand. The rain felt very honoured but modestly bowed his head and said: „There is someone who is still mightier than me. When he is blowing he splits up my clouds and scares me of the whole world. It's the wind." „So I have to ask the wind!", father mouse said and went in search for him. After long ways he finally met the wind and said: „Wind, you certainly are the mightiest man of all, mightier than the rain, mightier than the master of the sun, you are the desired groom for our daughter!" The wind was very pleased about the proposal but sighed and said: „I wished it were as you say. But there is someone, when he bars my way, I cannot get any further and have to evade. The mountain you are standing on is mightier than me."
And father mouse tumbled down the mountain with fright.

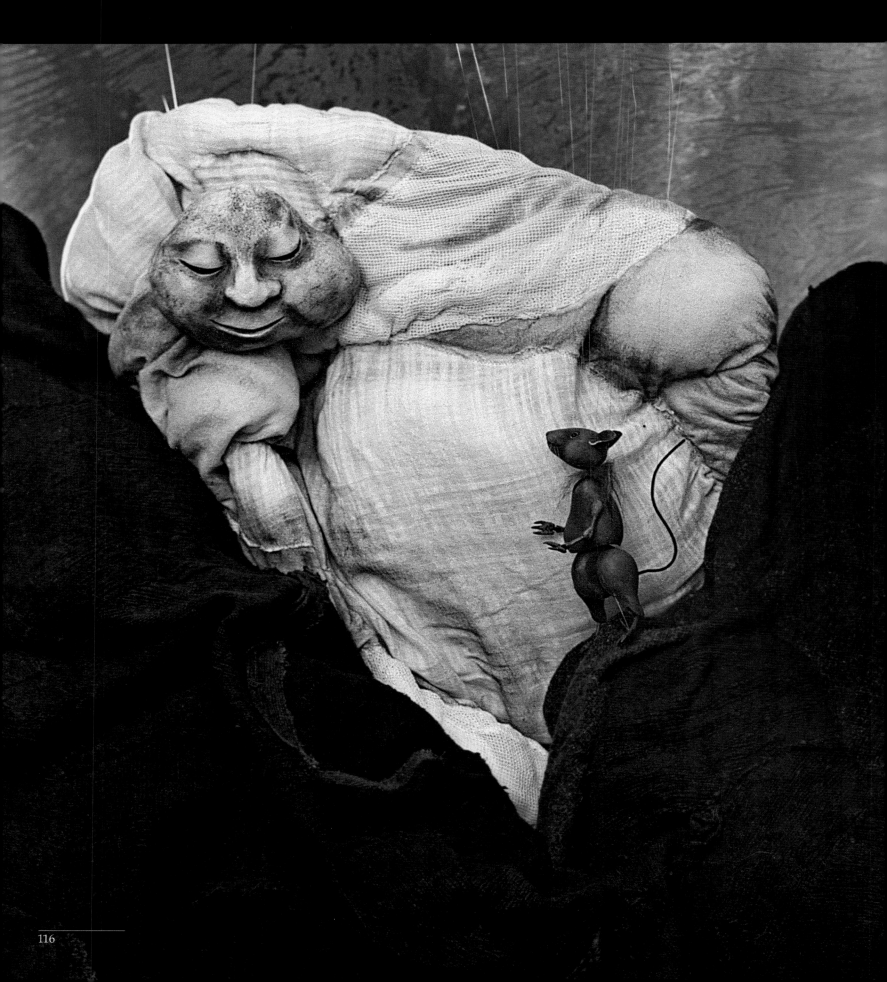

Doch er stieg sogleich wieder hinauf und rief: „Großer Berg, du Mächtiger! Wir wollen unsere Tochter nur mit dem großartigsten Mann verheiraten und so trage ich dir die Hand unserer Tochter an!" „Danke, dass du für deine Tochter an mich gedacht hast!", sagte der Berg. „Aber meine Macht reicht nicht heran an die Macht eines Volkes dort unten in der Tiefe." Und der Berg schaute hinab. „Siehst du all die vielen Löcher in meinem Sockel? Ich werde bald in Millionen von kleinen Felsstückchen zerfallen. Dort ist der Ort, wo du nach dem mächtigen Bräutigam für deine Tochter suchen musst." Papa Maus schaute genau hin und entdeckte, wer die vielen Löcher gegraben hatte – Mäuse! „Wer hätte gedacht, dass die Mäuse die Besten und Großartigsten von der ganzen Welt sind!", sagte Papa Maus. „Das muss ich meiner Familie erzählen." Er lief nach Hause und erzählte seiner Frau und seiner Tochter die Geschichten vom Sonnenherrn, vom Regen mit seiner dunklen Wolke, vom Wind, vom Berg und von den Mäusen. Die Tochter freute sich, denn sie wollte schon immer einen hübschen Mäuserich heiraten.

Und so wurde eine große Hochzeit gefeiert.

Eine Mythe aus Birma

But at once he climbed up again and cried: „Great mountain, you mighty man! We want our daughter to marry only the most splendid man and so I offer you our daughter's hand." „Thank you for thinking of me in this matter!", the mountain said. „But my power does not measure up to the power of a nation down there in the depth." And the mountain looked down. „Can you see all those holes in my base. Soon I will crumble into many small pieces of rock. Down there is the place where you should go in search for the mighty groom for your daughter." Father mouse looked carefully and recognized who had digged the many holes: Mice! „Who would have ever thought that mice were the best and most splendid creatures of the world!", father mouse exclaimed. „I have to go and tell my family."
He hurried home and told his wife and daughter the story of the master of the sun, of the rain with his dark cloud, of the wind, of the mountain and of the mice.
The daughter was happy because she had always wanted to marry a handsome mouse man.
And so they celebrated a great wedding.

A myth from Burma

Das kleine Mädchen mit den Schwefelhölzchern

The little girl with the matches

Es war entsetzlich kalt, es schneite und der letzte Abend des Jahres begann zu dunkeln. In dieser Kälte und Dunkelheit ging auf der Straße ein kleines Mädchen mit bloßem Kopf und bloßen Füßen, die rot und blau vor Kälte waren. In seiner Schürze trug es eine Menge Schwefelhölzchen und ein Bund davon in der Hand. Aus allen Fenstern glänzten die Lichter und es roch in der Straße herrlich nach Gänsebraten; es war ja Silvesterabend.

In einem Winkel zwischen zwei Häusern setzte es sich hin und kauerte sich zusammen, aber es fror noch mehr. Nach Hause zu gehen wagte es nicht. Es hatte ja keine Schwefelhölzchen verkauft und nicht einen Schilling bekommen. Sein Vater würde es schlagen und kalt war es zu Hause auch.

Die kleinen Hände waren beinahe vor Kälte erstarrt. Ach! Ein Schwefelhölzchen könnte ihm guttun, wenn es sich daran die Finger wärmen dürfte: Es zog eins heraus, „Ritsch", wie brannte es! Es war eine warme helle Flamme, als es die Hände darüber hielt. Es schien dem kleinen Mädchen, als säße es vor einem großen eisernen Ofen. Das Feuer brannte so schön und es wärmte so gut! Das Mädchen streckte schon die Füße aus, um sie zu wärmen – da erlosch die Flamme, der Ofen verschwand, es hatte nur den Rest des Schwefelhölzchens in der Hand. Ein neues wurde angestrichen, und wo der Schein auf die Mauer fiel, wurde diese durchsichtig. Es konnte gerade in die Stube hineinsehen, wo der Tisch fein gedeckt war und die gebratene Gans herrlich dampfte.

Und – die Gans sprang von der Schüssel herunter und wackelte auf dem Fußboden gerade auf das Mädchen zu. Da erlosch das Schwefelhölzchen und nur die kalte Mauer war zu sehen.

Es zündete noch ein Hölzchen an. Da saß es nun unter dem herrlichsten Weihnachtsbaum. Tausende von Lichtern brannten auf den Zweigen. Das kleine Mädchen streckte die Hände danach aus – da erlosch das Schwefelhölzchen. Die Weihnachtslichter jedoch stiegen höher und höher und es sah sie jetzt als helle Sterne am Himmel; einer von ihnen fiel herunter und bildete einen Feuerschweif am Himmel.

„Jetzt stirbt jemand", sagte das kleine Mäd-

It was dreadfully cold, it was snowing, and night was starting to fall on the last day of the year. Amid this cold and darkness, a little girl walked along the street, bare-headed and with bare feet that were red and blue with cold. In her apron she carried a quantity of matches, and she also bore a bundle in her hand. Lights gleamed from every window, and the street was filled with the wonderful fragrance of roasting goose; it was, after all, New Year's Eve. In a nook formed by two houses, she sat down and huddled herself up, but she froze even worse. She dare not go home, for she had sold no matches and earned not a single penny. Her father would beat her, and anyway, it was cold at home, too. Her little hands were almost stiff with cold. Oh! A match would be so comforting if only she could warm her fingers on one: She drew one out. "Scratch," and how it burned! It was a warm, bright flame, as she held her hands over it. It seemed to the little girl as though she sat before a great iron stove. The fire burned so brightly and it warmed so wonderfully! The little girl was just stretching out her feet to warm them – when the flame went out, the stove vanished, and she only had the remains of the match in her hand.

She struck a new one, and where the light fell on the wall, it became transparent. The little girl could see straight into the room, where the table was beautifully set and the roast goose was steaming famously.

And all of a sudden, the goose sprang down from the dish and waddled across the floor straight towards the little girl. But then the match went out, and all that was to be seen was the cold wall.

The little girl lit another match. This time she was sitting under the most magnificent Christmas tree. Thousands of lights were burning on its branches. The little girl reached her hands out towards them – and the match went out. The Christmas lights, however, rose higher and higher, and she now saw them as bright stars in the sky, one of which fell down and formed a trail of fire in the sky.

chen, denn die verstorbene Großmutter hatte ihm erzählt, dass, wenn ein Stern vom Himmel herabfällt, eine Seele zu Gott emporsteigt.

Es strich wieder ein Hölzchen an, es leuchtete und in dem Glanze stand die alte Großmutter, so mild und liebevoll.

„Großmutter", rief die Kleine. „Oh, nimm mich mit! Ich weiß, du bist fort, wenn das Schwefel-hölzchen erlischt, genau wie der Ofen, die Gans oder der Weihnachtsbaum."

Und es strich schnell den ganzen Rest der Schwefelhölzchen an, denn es wollte die Groß-mutter recht festhalten. Die Schwefelhölzchen leuchteten. Großmutter war früher nie so schön, so groß gewesen. Sie nahm das kleine Mädchen in ihre Arme und sie flogen in Glanz und Freude so hoch, so hoch. Dort oben waren weder Kälte noch Hunger, noch Angst – sie waren im Frieden.

Aber im Winkel des Hauses saß das kleine Mädchen mit roten Wangen und lächelndem Munde – tot, erfroren an des alten Jahres letzten Abend. Der Neujahrsmorgen ging über dem toten Kinde auf, das dort mit den abge-brannten Schwefelhölzchen saß. „Es hat sich erwärmen wollen", sagte man.

Niemand wusste, was es Schönes gesehen hat-te, in welchem Glanze es mit der Großmutter zur Neujahrsfreude eingegangen war.

Nach Hans Christian Andersen

"Now someone will be dying," said the little girl, for her grandmother, who was now dead, had told her that whenever a star falls from the sky, a soul ascends to God.

She struck another match; it flared, and in its light stood her old grandmother, so kind and full of love.

"Grandmother," the little one cried, "Oh, take me with you! I know you will disappear when the match goes out, just like the stove, the goose and the Christmas tree."

And she quickly lit all the remaining matches, so much did she want to keep her grandmother with her. The matches shone. Grandmother had never before been so beautiful, so tall. She took the little girl in her arms, and they flew in brightness and joy so high, so very high; – and up there, there was neither cold, nor hunger nor fear – they were in peace.

In the nook between the houses, however, sat the little girl, with red cheeks and a smiling mouth – dead, frozen on the last evening of the year. New Year's morning arose over the dead child, sitting there with her burnt-down matches. "She sought to warm herself," people said.

No one knew what beautiful things she had seen, nor the splendour in which she had gone with her grandmother to the joys of the New Year.

by Hans Christian Andersen

Eines Tages öffnete Peter die Gartentür und ging hinaus auf die große grüne Wiese ...

One day, Peter opened the garden gate and went out into the great green meadow ...

125

Draußen ist es bitterkalt.
Es schneit und weht ein kalter
Wind. Immer wieder klopft es
bei Wanja in der Nacht. Nach-
einander bitten ein Hase, ein
Fuchs und ein Bär um Einlass
und Wärme. Aber wird nicht
etwa der Fuchs den Hasen
fressen? Und der Bär den
Fuchs?

Outside, it's bitterly cold. It's
snowing, and there's an icy
wind blowing. In the night,
there are repeated knocks on
Vanya's door. One by one, a
hare, a fox and a bear ask to
be allowed in to warm themselves up. But won't the fox
eat the hare? And won't the
bear eat the fox?

stellt sich vor, was für ein guter Bärenvater er doch wäre. Aber er weiß nicht, wie das gehen soll. Er nimmt all seinen Mut zusammen und ruft in den Wald hinein ... und bekommt von vielen Tieren ebenso viele Antworten.
Bis auf einmal ... ja, was denn nun?

and thinks what a good bear father he would make. But he doesn't know how to set about it. So he plucks up all his courage and shouts into the forest ... and receives replies from many animals, but each one different.
Until suddenly ... yes, what?

Das Eselein

The little donkey

Es waren einmal ein König ...

Once upon a time there were a king ...

... und eine Königin.

... and a queen.

Es lebten einmal ein König und eine Königin, die waren reich und hatten alles, was sie sich wünschten, nur keine Kinder. Endlich erfüllte Gott ihre Wünsche; als das Kind aber zur Welt kam, war es ein junges Eselein. Wie die Mutter das erblickte, wollte sie lieber gar kein Kind; der König aber sprach: „Nein, hat Gott ihn gegeben, soll er auch mein Sohn und Erbe sein." Das Eselein wuchs auf, sprang herum, spielte und hatte besonders seine Lust an der Musik, sodass es zu einem berühmten Spielmann in die Lehre ging und bald seine Laute schlagen konnte wie der Meister selbst. Einmal ging das Herrlein nachdenksam spazieren und kam an einen Brunnen, da schaute es hinein und sah im spiegelhellen Wasser seine Eseleinsgestalt. Darüber war es so betrübt, dass es in die weite Welt ging und nur seine Laute mitnahm. Es

zog auf und ab; zuletzt kam es in ein Reich, wo ein alter König herrschte, der nur eine einzige, aber wunderschöne Tochter hatte.

Once upon a time there were a king and a queen who mere rich and had anything they ever hoped for except children. God finally repelled this wish; but when the child was born it was a little donkey. As the mother saw it, she would have prefered to have no child at all, but the king said: "No, God gave it to us so shall it be my son and heir." The little donkey grew up, leaped around, played and especially enjoyed music so that it served its apprenticeship under a famous musician and soon could play its lute like the master himself.
Once the young donkey walked thoughtfully and came to a well, it looked into it und saw its little donkey build in the shining water. It was so sad about this sight that it set out into the big wide world and only took the lute with it. It wandered around and finally came to an empire ruled by an old king who only had one single but lovely daughter.
At first its admittance was refused but the little donkey played the lute most wonderfully and knew to behave so distinguishedly and well that it was allowed to sit at the royal table next to the beautiful princess herself.
When the noble little animal had spent a good while at the royal house it thought, „What can I do about it. I have to return home." And it sadly hung its head, went to the king and required its dismissal.

Der Diener
erzählte dem
König alles ...

The servant
told the king
everything ...

... und riet
dem König,
die nächste
Nacht selbst zu
wachen.

... and recom-
mended that
the king himself
should keep
watch the next
night.

Erst wollte man es nicht einlassen, aber das Eselein schlug die Laute auf das Schönste und wusste sich so fein und artig zu betragen, dass es an der königlichen Tafel neben der schönen Königstochter selbst sitzen durfte. Als das edle Tierchen eine gute Zeit an des Königs Hof geblieben war, dachte es: „Was hilft das alles, du musst wieder heim", ließ den Kopf traurig hängen, trat vor den König und verlangte seinen Abschied. Der König hatte es aber lieb gewonnen und sprach: „Eselein, was ist mit dir; bleib bei mir; ich will dir geben, was du verlangst. Willst du Gold?" „Nein", sagte das Eselein und schüttelte mit dem Kopf. „Willst du Kostbarkeiten und Schmuck?" „Nein". „Willst du mein halbes Reich?" „Nein". Da sprach der König: „Wenn ich nur wüsste, was dich vergnügt machen könnte. Willst du meine schöne Tochter zur Frau?" „Ach ja", sagte das Eselein, „die möchte ich wohl haben", war auf einmal ganz lustig und guter Dinge, denn das war's gerade, was es sich gewünscht hatte.
Nun ward eine große und prächtige Hochzeit gefeiert. Abends, wie Braut und Bräutigam in ihr Schlafkämmerlein geführt wurden, wollte der König wissen, ob sich das Eselein auch fein manierlich und artig betrüge und hieß einen Diener, sich dort zu verstecken. Wie sie nun beide drinnen waren, schob der Bräutigam den Riegel vor die Türe, blickte sich um, und wie er glaubte, dass sie ganz allein wären, da warf er auf einmal seine Eselshaut ab und stand da als ein schöner königlicher Jüngling.

But the king had grown fond of it and said: „Little donkey, what's up with you; stay with me, I will give you any thing you want. Do you want gold?" „No", the little donkey replied and shook its head. „Do you want treasures and jewellery?" „No". „Do you want half of my empire?" „Oh no". Thereupon the king said: „If I only knew what would make you happy. Do you want to take my beautiful daughter for your wife?" „Oh yes", the little donkey said. „I would really like to take her" and all of a sudden it was entirely cheerful and happy, because that exactly was what it had wished for.

The task of the marionette artist is to render
the poetry of the world visible as purely
as possible in the materials.
Image, gesture, action – nothing more.
Tankred Dorst

Now they had a great and splendid wedding. In the evening, when bride and groom were led to their bedroom, the king wanted to know whether the little donkey would behave respectably and well and told his servant to hide there. As they both were inside, the groom bolted the door, looked around and when it believed that they were all by themselves it suddenly throw of its donkey skin and stood there as a beautiful royal youth.

Da stand ein
schöner königli-
cher Jüngling ...

There stood a
beautiful royal
youth ...

... und die Prin-
zessin war froh,
küsste ihn und
hatte ihn von
Herzen lieb.

... and the
princess was
very happy,
kissed him and
loved him with
all her heart.

„Nun siehst du", sprach er, „wer ich bin, und
siehst auch, dass ich deiner nicht unwert war."
Da ward die Braut froh, küsste ihn und hatte
ihn von Herzen lieb. Als aber der Morgen her-
ankam, sprang er auf, zog seine Tierhaut wieder über und kein Mensch hätte gedacht, was
für einer dahintersteckte. Der Diener erzählte
dem König alles und riet ihm, die nächste
Nacht selbst zu wachen, die Eselshaut zu nehmen und sie zu verbrennen. Dem König gefiel
der Rat und als der Jüngling eingeschlafen war,
ging er in die Kammer, nahm die Haut, ließ ein
großes Feuer machen und verbrannte sie und
wachte die ganze Nacht.
Als der Jüngling ausgeschlafen hatte, stand er
auf und wollte die Eselshaut anziehen, aber sie
war nicht zu finden. Da wollte er entfliehen.
Wie er hinaustrat, stand aber der König da und
sprach: „Mein Sohn, wohin so eilig? Bleib hier,
du bist ein so schöner Mann, du sollst nicht
wieder von mir. Ich gebe dir jetzt mein halbes
Reich und nach meinem Tod bekommst du es
ganz." „So wünsch ich, dass der gute Anfang
auch ein gutes Ende nehme", sprach der Jüngling, „ich bleibe bei Euch." Da gab ihm der
Alte das halbe Reich und als er nach einem
Jahr starb, hatte er das ganze und nach dem
Tod seines Vaters noch eins dazu und lebte
in aller Herrlichkeit.

Ein Märchen der Brüder Grimm

„Now you can see", he said, „who I am and
you can recognize that I have been worthy of
you." Thereupon the bride was very happy,
kissed him and loved him with all her heart.
But when the morning came he jumped to his
feet, put on his animal skin again and nobody
would have ever thought who would be un-
derneath. The servant told the king everything
and recommended that the king himself should
keep watch the next night, take the donkey
skin and burn it. The king liked this advice and
when the youth had fallen asleep he went into
the room, took the skin, ordered a great fire to
be made and burn the skin and kept watch the
whole night.
After a good sleep the youth stood up and
wanted to put on the donkey skin but couldn't
find it. So he wanted to flee. But when he went
out the king was there and said: „Son, where
are you going to so hastily? Stay here, you are
such a beautiful man, yon shall not leave me
again. Half of my empire I will give to you now
and after my death you will get the other half,
too." „So I wish that the good beginning shall
also come to a good end", the youth said: „I
will stay with you." Now the old man gave him
half the empire and when he died a year later
he got the complete empire and after the death
of his father still another one und lived on in
splendour.

A fairy tale by the Brothers Grimm

... und sie lebten in aller Herrlichkeit.

... and they lived on in splendour.

Him, der Bär, in Kappadokien

Him, the bear, in Cappadocia

Mitten im Morgenland, auf dem Zweizacken-berg in Kappadokien, findet eine deutsch-türki-sche Hochzeit statt. Aus der ganzen Welt reisen die Gäste an. Auch Him, der Bär, macht sich auf den weiten Weg. Mit dem Orient-Express reist er nach Istanbul. Überwältigt vom bunten Treiben schlendert er durch das Gewimmel der Großstadt, besucht neugierig eine Moschee und den Bazar. Auf der Suche nach einem Hochzeitsgeschenk kauft er von seinem letzten Geld eine köstliche Torte. Stolz und vorsichtig balanciert er sie durch das Gedränge, setzt sie behutsam auf einer Parkbank ab und ruht sich erschöpft aus. Da nähert sich ein großer Mann und plumpst – ganz in seine Zeitung vertieft – mit seinem dicken Hintern mitten in die kost-bare Torte. Der Bär ist verzweifelt! Jetzt hat er weder Geld noch Hochzeitsgeschenk.
Betrübt schläft er ein.

Deep in the Orient, on Two-Peaks Mountain in Cappadocia, a German-Turkish wedding is set to take place. Guests are invited from all over the world. Him, the Bear, also sets off on the long journey. First, he travels on the Orient Express to Istanbul. Thrilled by the sights and sounds, he explores the bustle of the great city, also visiting a mosque and a bazaar. Looking for a suitable wedding gift, he spends the last of his money on a delicious cake. He proudly and carefully carries it through the crowds, then places it gently on a park bench and sits himself down beside it for a rest. A large man approaches, engrossed in his newspaper, and also plonks his large behind down on the bench, right in the precious cake. Him, the Bear, is in despair. He now has no money, and no wedding present either.
Sadly, he falls asleep.

Da erscheint ihm ein Djinn und setzt ihn auf
einen fliegenden Teppich. Er fliegt über atem-
beraubende Landschaften und landet in den
fantastisch geformten Weiten Kappadokiens.
In der Ferne erkennt Him den Zweizackenberg
und macht sich auf den mühsamen Weg. Er
kommt durch tiefe Schluchten, verläuft sich in
bizarr geformten Höhlen und überwindet wag-
halsig selbst steilste Höhen. Endlich hört er in
der Ferne Musik und Kinderlachen. Die Hochzeit hat schon begonnen und er wird begeistert aufgenommen in einem lustigen, überaus
bunten Hochzeitstreiben. Alle freuen sich, dass
Him, der Bär, den weiten, weiten Weg geschafft
hat. Sein Kommen ist das schönste Geschenk,
das er dem Brautpaar machen kann.

*Dieser zwanzigminütige Film entstand in Zusam-
menarbeit mit der Filmemacherin Alkeste Wegner
aus Uchisar/Kappadokien.*
www.pendel-marionetten.de

Suddenly, a genie appears and places him on
a flying carpet. He flies over breathtaking land-
scapes and finally lands amid the vast, fantas-
tically formed landscape of Cappadocia. In the
distance, he recognizes Two-Peaks Mountain
and sets off on the arduous route to get there,
passing through deep gorges, getting lost in
bizarrely shaped caves and daringly climbing
even the steepest inclines along the way. At
last, he hears the sounds of music and laughing
children. The wedding has already started,
and he is welcomed with joy into the merry,
colourful festivities. Everyone is delighted that
Him, the Bear, has accomplished this long, long
journey.

*This twenty-minute film was created in collaborati-
on with film maker Alkeste Wegner
of Uchisar/Cappadocia.*
www.pendel-marionetten.de

Biografie

Marlene Gmelin und Detlef Schmelz beschäftigen sich seit den 1970er-Jahren mit Marionetten. Damals, während ihres Pädagogik-Studiums in Marburg, lebten sie in einer Wohngemeinschaft auf einem Bauernhof und träumten zusammen mit Gleichgesinnten von einem unabhängigen Leben als Selbstversorger. Um das zu verwirklichen, entstanden viele kleine Werkstätten, unter anderem eine erste Biobäckerei und eine Drechslerei. Sie beide widmeten sich dem Marionettenbau. In diesem kreativen Umfeld entstand ein studentisches Marionettentheater. Marlene Gmelin und Detlef Schmelz erlebten die Wirkung der Marionette auf Zuschauer und Spieler und ahnten, dass in diesem geheimnisvollen Wesen viel mehr Tiefe steckt als vermutet.

1974 wurde ihre Wohngemeinschaft zu einer Ausstellung über alternative Projekte in Schwäbisch-Hall eingeladen. Dort lernten sie Fritz Herbert Bross kennen, den künstlerischen Leiter von Gerhards Marionetten und Koryphäe auf dem Gebiet der Marionette. Dieser betrachtete die Marionette sehr komplex und sah in ihr auf ideale Weise die verschiedensten Künste und Wissenschaften mit filigranem Handwerk vereint. Von ihm bekamen sie sehr wertvolle Anregungen für den Marionettenbau und das Marionettenspiel. Er prägte ihre Sicht auf dieses Medium. Leider verstarb er, bevor sie eine Lehre bei ihm beginnen konnten. Nach dem Studium lebten sie für ein Jahr in Griechenland, hatten dort zwei Esel und viel Zeit zum Nachdenken; es festigte sich der Wunsch, die Marionettenkunst von der Pike auf zu erlernen. 1979, von Griechenland aus, vereinbarten sie mit Ingmar Kaeser, einem langjährigen Schüler von F. H. Bross, eine dreijährige Ausbildung. Diese fand bei Gerhards Marionetten in Schwäbisch Hall statt. Später übernahm Marlene Gmelin die künstlerische Leitung dieser Bühne und Detlef Schmelz spezialisierte sich auf die technische Umsetzung und die Anfertigung von Tierfiguren. Über das Restaurieren alter Figuren und Neuanfertigungen zur Ergänzung alter Stücke haben sie posthum noch viel von F. H. Bross gelernt.

Biography

While studying education in the mid-1970s, Marlene Gmelin and Detlef Schmelz were living in a farmhouse near Marburg which they shared with other people. The dream of the farm dwellers was to live a life of independence and self-sufficiency. In fulfilment of that goal, they set up a number of small workshops. Marlene Gmelin and Detlef Schmelz turned to marionette making. This developed into a student theatre, and they soon came to recognize that marionettes are enigmatic beings, with much greater depth than at first sight appears to be the case. At an exhibition devoted to alternative projects, held in 1974 in Schwäbisch-Hall, they were introduced to Fritz Herbert Bross, the artistic director of Gerhards Marionette Theatre and a leading light in the world of marionettes. He saw marionettes as a synthesis of various arts and sciences, plus the most delicate manual craftsmanship. He gave them many very valuable ideas for marionette making and marionette playing. Sadly, he died before they were able to begin an apprenticeship with him.

Having finished their study courses, they lived for a year in Greece, with two donkeys and much time for thinking; and the wish gradually took hold of them to learn the art of marionetteering from the bottom up. In 1979, while still in Greece, they agreed on a three-year programme of training with Ingmar Kaeser, a long-standing pupil of F. H. Bross. They undertook this at Gerhards Marionetten in Schwäbisch Hall. By restoring old figures and making new parts to complete old items, they still learned a lot from F. H. Bross posthumously. Marlene Gmelin took over the artistic direction of the theatre, while Detlef Schmelz specialized in the technical realization and the production of animal figures.

In 1990, the two of them initially set up in business as marionette makers, under the name "Pendel". Their marionettes won them national and international awards. They soon came to realize that marionette making and marionette playing are inseparable. In 1991, therefore, they founded their own touring theatre, starting with a programme of scenes entitled "Stories without Words".

1990 machten sie sich unter dem Namen „Pendel" als Marionettenbildner selbstständig. Für ihre Marionetten erhielten sie nationale und internationale Preise.

Bald merkten sie, dass der Marionettenbau sich nicht vom Marionettenspiel trennen lässt. Deshalb gründeten sie 1991 ihr eigenes Tourneetheater, das mit der Inszenierung des Szenenprogramms „Geschichten ohne Worte" begann. Insbesondere mit diesem Stück sind sie in vielen Ländern und Kontinenten aufgetreten. Gemeinsam mit der Erzählerin der Europäischen Märchengesellschaft, Margarete Möckel, entstand danach das Grimm'sche Märchen „Das Eselein" sowie „Die Mäusebraut", eine Mythe aus Birma.

Ihre Inszenierungen wenden sich gleichermaßen an Erwachsene wie an Kinder. Das pantomimische Spiel steht immer im Vordergrund, auch bei den Märchen. In der Regel leiten nur wenige Worte das Geschehen ein, dann entwickelt sich das Marionettenspiel zu Musik, so wie bei „Ben, der Bär, und die Traumfischsegler", einer poetischen Reise um die Welt, die in einer fulminanten Zirkusveranstaltung endet. Dieses Stück entstand 2002 in Zusammenarbeit mit dem Komponisten und Erzähler Gregory Charamsa, der auch die Musik für „Das Eselein" komponierte.

Für „Das kleine Mädchen mit den Schwefelhölzchen" wählten sie 2008 eine besondere Aufführungsform: Das Märchen wird vorab erzählt und dann pantomimisch zu Musik aufgeführt. Es folgte eine sehr aufwendige Inszenierung mit vielen Beteiligten: die Einstudierung von „Peter und der Wolf". Hier verschmelzen Sprache, Musik und Spiel zu einem Ganzen, denn das Marionettenspiel wird begleitet von dem Rezitator Eduard Gruber und dem Frankfurter Bläserensemble Flexibilé.

In all dieser Zeit bauten sie ihr altes Bauernhaus weiter aus und richteten sich dort 2007 ihr eigenes Theater ein: östlich der Sonne und westlich vom Mond. Es ist klein und fein - die Vorstellungen darin sind von einer besonderen Intensität. Der Spielplan dort konzentriert sich auf die Wintermonate, während das Tournéetheater das ganze Jahr über unterwegs ist.

Detlef Schmelz mit Him, dem Bären, in den Felsen Kapatokiens.

Detlef Schmelz with Him, the Bear, amidst the rocks of Cappadocia.

By now, they have presented this work, in particular, in many countries all over the world. In collaboration with Margarete Möckel, narrator at the European Fairytale Society (Europäische Märchengesellschaft), this was followed by Grimms' fairy tale "The Little Donkey", and the "Mouse Bride", a myth from Burma. Right from the start, their productions were aimed at children and adults alike. Mime always played the dominant role, even in the fairy tales. As a rule, only a few words are spoken at the beginning in order to set the scene, and then, accompanied by music, the marionette show takes over, as in "Ben the Bear and the Dream Fish Sailors", a poetic journey around the world that ends in an exuberant circus show. This work was created in 2002 in cooperation with the composer and narrator Gregory Charamsa, who also wrote the music for "The Little Donkey". For "The Little Girl with the Matches", they chose a different form of presentation, the story being told in advance and then performed in mime to music. A further development step was the production of "Peter and the Wolf". Here, speech, music and acting amalgamate to form a whole, with the marionette playing accompanied by the narration of Eduard Gruber and music played by the Frankfurt wind ensemble Flexibilé. Over the years, they have renovated their old farmhouse, which since 2007 has also housed their own theatre, with space for around 40 spectators.

Marlene Gmelin
spielt im Süden
Ruandas vor be-
geisterter Dorf-
bevölkerung.

Marlene Gmelin
plays before
an enthusiastic
village audience
in southern
Rwanda.

Seit 1995 halten Marlene Gmelin und Detlef
Schmelz regelmäßig Seminare, in denen sie die
Kunst des Marionettenspiels lehren. Daraus
entstanden in Deutschland und den Nach-
barstaaten Spielinitiativen und Theater. Viele
der Spielkursteilnehmer haben heute eigene
Bühnen und tragen so zum Fortbestand des
Marionettentheaters bei. Mit ihnen gemeinsam
findet seit 2008 alle zwei Jahre das Pendel-Marionetten-Festival statt. Es zeigt die unendliche
Vielfalt und den Zauber des Marionettenspiels.
Höhepunkt eines jeden Festivals ist ein großes
Gemeinschaftsstück, das jeweils neu erarbeitet
wird. 2012 war das unter dem Eindruck ver-
schiedener Krisen in der realen Welt ein Stück
über den Umgang der Menschen mit dem Klima und der Umwelt: „Ein paar Grad plus".

Mit dieser Lehrtätigkeit schließt sich der Kreis
zwischen Pädagogikstudium und der inten-
siven Beschäftigung mit der Marionette.

The performances in this setting have a special
intensity. The scheduled performances mostly
take place in the winter months, but special
performances can also be booked for special
occasions.

A regular features of Marlene Gmelin and
Detlef Schmelz's activities since 1995 have been
training courses in which they pass on the joy
they take in marionetteering. These courses
have also led to the establishment of playing
initiatives and theatres in both Germany and
neighbouring countries. Many former course
participants now have their own stages, hel-
ping to ensure the future of marionette theatre.
In collaboration with them, and first launched
in 2008, the Pendel-Marionette-Festival is now
held every two years. This provides a platform
for the endless variety and magic of marionette
theatre. The highlight of each festival is a large-
scale joint work, developed in the training
courses over a period of around two years.

Das Pendel-
Marionetten-
Theater in
Ingelfingen-
Hermuthausen

The Pendel-
Marionette-
Theatre in
Ingelfingen-
Hermuthausen

© 2013 Marionetten · Kunst, Bau, Spiel | Marionettes · Art, Construction, Play
Marlene Gmelin und Detlef Schmelz
Swiridoff Verlag GmbH & Co. KG, Goethestraße 14, D-74653 Künzelsau
ISBN 978-3-89929-281-7
3. Auflage, komplett neu überarbeitet | 3rd Edition, revised

Texte | Texts Marlene Gmelin: 42 – 49,
Detlef Schmelz: 18 – 40, 50 – 57, 78 – 95, 98 – 100, 136 – 138
Marlene Gmelin und Detlef Schmelz: 8 – 9, 58 – 77, 101 – 134, 144 – 147
Ingrid Riedel: 10 – 17 (in Anlehnung an „Die vier Elemente im Traum" | in dependense on „The four elements in a dream", Walter Verlag AG, Zürich und Düsseldorf)

Fotos | Pictures Hildegard Wegner: Umschlag/-rückseite, 12, 13, 14, 17↑→, 23, 24, 25, 28, 29, 31, 33, 39, 45↑, 46, 48↑← ↓←, 49↓→, 56←, 60, 61, 62, 63, 64, 65, 66, 70, 73, 99, 100/101, 102, 103, 104, 105, 107, 113, 115, 116, 117, 118, 119, 126/127
Marlene Gmelin und Detlef Schmelz: 5, 6, 7, 9, 16, 17, 19, 32, 35, 37, 41, 43, 44, 45↓, 48↑→,↓→, 49↑ ↑←, 51 – 55, 56→, 68←, 68→, 71, 74, 76, 77, 79↓, 80↓→, 86/87, 89, 90/91, 92, 97↑→, 108/109, 111/112, 121, 122, 123, 124/125, 128/129, 130, 131, 132, 133, 134, 135, 145, 147←
Cordula Sachs: 80↓←, 81↓→, 83, 84↑→, 85↓←, 93, 95, 96/97
Bernhard Betz: 78→, 80, 81↕ ↓←, 82→, 83, 84, 85, 88, 94
Thomas Cleve: 21, 56↕, 68/69↕, 72, 78←, 79↑, 81, 82←
Ahmet Teke: 136 – 143
Marlies Hilburg-Schmelz: 10, 11
Gabriele Bothen-Hack: 15, 47
Gottfried Keller: 59, 147→
Uli Gebhard: 75, 97↑←
Lilo Mangelsdorff: 85↕→
Edith Nikel: 81↑→
Klaus-Peter Steffe: 27
Gesine Eising: 142

Zeichnungen | Graphics Marlene Gmelin, 58 – 65
Bildbearbeitung | Image processing Marlene Gmelin, Thomas Cleve

Gestaltung | Design Gottfried Keller, Basel
Übersetzung | Translation Terber und Partner, Münster
Gabriele Kahn, Uslar, 102
Lektorat | Editing Claudia Kohlenberger, Weikersheim
Druck | Printing W. Kohlhammer, Stuttgart

Wir danken herzlich
Hildegard Wegner, der Lichtbildnerin.
Von ihr stammen viele Fotos. Sie hat unser Auge für das eigene Fotografieren geschult.
Gottfried Keller, dem Gestalter.
Unverhofft kam er in unser Leben – und hat in endlosen Stunden das schöne Layout erstellt.
Claudia Kohlenberger, der Lektorin.
Sie half entscheidend, die Texte in die richtige Form zu bringen.
Thomas Cleve, dem Helfer.
Ob in technischen oder gestalterischen Fragen – er ist wesentlich an diesem Buch beteiligt.
Carmen Würth,
die die Idee zum Buchprojekt unterstützt und den Kontakt zum Verlag hergestellt hat.
All unseren Spielkursteilnehmern.

Our thanks go in particular to
Hildegard Wegner, the photographer,
by whom many of the photos in this book were taken and who has sharpened our own eyes for photography.
Gottfried Keller, the designer,
who came into our lives out of the blue and spent endless hours creating the wonderful layout you now see.
Claudia Kohlenberger, the editor,
who played an invaluable role in knocking the texts in this book into the proper shape.
Thomas Cleve, right-hand man and expert in all technical and creative matters,
who has been closely involved in the creation of this book.
Carmen Würth,
who supported the idea for this book project and established the contact to the publishers.
All participants in our marionette courses.

Pendel

Marionetten · Kunst, Bau, Spiel
Pendel-Marionettentheater
Marlene Gmelin und Detlef Schmelz
Ratsgasse 15 · D 74653 Ingelfingen-Hermuthausen
Telefon 0049/7940-3694
www.pendel-marionetten.de · info@pendel-marionetten.de
Sondervorstellungen auf Anfrage möglich | Special performances on request possible